Measuring Up on the New York State Test

Mathematics
Grade 4

Developed specifically for the New York State Test

Measuring Up on the New York State Test Series includes instructional work texts
that match the English/Language Arts and Mathematics Standards for
Grades 3, 4, 7, and 8.

D1315174

The Peoples Publishing Group

Serving the Needs of New York Educators and Students

Visit our web site at:

http://www.nytesthelp.com

Permissions
p. 3, illustration by Steve Sullivan.
p. 70, 120, illustration by Armando Baez.

The Peoples Publishing Group, Inc. expresses its thanks to all the people who helped to create this book.

Editorial Development, ELHI Publishers Services

Pre-Press & Production Manager, Doreen Smith

Design, Infinite Ideas & Designs

New York Reviewer, Chris Herte, Finley M.S., Glen Cove, NY

Cover Design, Armando Baéz

Illustrators, Armando Baéz, Steve Sullivan

Technical Art, Brian W. Bishop, Andrea Bosiger, Infinite Ideas & Designs

ISBN 1-56256-310-6

Letter to Students

Dear Student,

This year you will take a very important test in May. It is called *the New York State Mathematics Test*. You will do well on this test by preparing and practicing–just like you would for an important game or performance. The information and strategies in this book are specially designed to help you succeed on the test.

The test is given over three days. This is what it asks you to do:

Day 1 • Multiple-Choice Questions   **40 minutes**
You will answer 30 multiple-choice questions.

Day 2 • Open-Ended Questions   **50 minutes**
You will answer 7 short response questions and 2 extended response questions.

Day 3 • Open-Ended Questions   **50 minutes**
You will answer 7 short response questions and 2 extended response questions.

The practice you need for doing well on all of these areas is in this book. You will practice both mathematically and in writing—just like you will on the test. Each lesson gives you examples and helps you work through questions. Here are some things you should know about this book.

This picture means that you will need to use your ruler.

This picture means that you will need to use your pattern blocks.

This picture means that you will need to use your counters.

These activities can be completed at home. Take your book home and share what you are learning and practicing with your family.

Now it's time to get started. By the time you finish this book, you'll be ready and able for the test. Good luck!

The Table of Contents is an exact match to the Performance Indicators and Skills in the New York State Standards of Learning for Mathematics.

KEY IDEA 3 • OPERATIONS
Use mathematical operations and relationships among them to understand mathematics.

The Table of Contents is an exact match to the Performance Indicators and Skills in the New York State Standards of Learning for Mathematics.

The Table of Contents is an exact match to the Performance Indicators and Skills in the New York State Standards of Learning for Mathematics.

The Table of Contents is an exact match to the Performance Indicators and Skills in the New York State Standards of Learning for Mathematics.

KEY IDEA 7 • PATTERNS/FUNCTIONS
Use patterns and functions to develop mathematical power, appreciate the true beauty of mathematics, and construct generalizations that describe patterns simply and efficiently.

The Table of Contents is an exact match to the Performance Indicators and Skills in the New York State Standards of Learning for Mathematics.

The Table of Contents is an exact match to the Performance Indicators and Skills in the New York State Standards of Learning for Mathematics.

Lesson 1.1 • Factor and product relationships

> **READY REFERENCE**
> **factors** the numbers you multiply
> **product** the answer you get when you multiply factors
> **array** objects in rows and columns

 ## Think About It

Your teacher has asked you to count the jars of paint on each of the 4 shelves in the closet. Each shelf has 7 jars of paint on it. How many jars of paint are in the closet?

 ## Here's How

Addition	Multiplication
You can add the 7 jars on each shelf. $7 + 7 + 7 + 7 = 28$	When you need to add the same numbers over and over, you can multiply. 4 shelves × 7 jars on each shelf = 28 jars $4 \times 7 = 28$ *4 is a factor* *7 is a factor* *28 is the product*
You can use an array to show an addition sentence. $7 + 7 + 7 + 7 =$ _____	You can use an array to show a multiplication sentence. $4 \times 7 =$ _____ _____ is a factor. _____ is a factor. _____ is the product.

 **Practice**

Write one addition and one multiplication number sentence for each array or number line.

1

Addition   Multiplication

_____   _____

2 The factors are _____ and _____   **3** The product is _____.

4

Addition   Multiplication

_____   _____

5 The factors are _____ and _____.   **6** The product is _____.

Write a multiplication number sentence for each.

7 2 + 2 + 2 _____   **8** 4 + 4 + 4 + 4 _____

9 5 + 5 + 5 + 5 + 5 _____   **10** 8 + 8 + 8 _____

Short Response Question

11 Five shelves hold 6 books each. Draw an array to show the books on the shelves. Then write an addition sentence and a multiplication sentence to describe the books on the shelves. Explain how you wrote your number sentences.

Addition sentence _____

Multiplication sentence _____

_____

_____

Lesson 1.2 ▪ Statements that use *and*, *or*, and *not*

 Think About It

Katie, Megan, and Carl were three of the runners who entered the 50-meter dash on field day. Each was awarded a ribbon—blue for first place, red for second place, and yellow for third place. They each wore numbers on their shirts. Katie, wearing #23, did *not* win the first place ribbon. Carl did *not* come in third. Carl, wearing #11, finished just behind the runner who wore #17. Megan did *not* come in third. Who won each of the ribbons for first, second, and third place? What numbers did they wear?

 Here's How

Step 1 Create a picture in your mind about what you have read. Sometimes it is useful to draw a picture.

Step 2 List the facts.

1. Katie did *not* win first place.
2. Carl finished *after* the runner who wore #17, so Carl did *not* win.
3. Carl did *not* come in third.
4. Megan did *not* come in third.
5. Katie wore #23, and Carl wore #11.
6. Number 17 finished *before* Carl, so that runner could *not* have been third.

Step 3 Fill in a chart using the facts you know. Write *yes* if the fact is true. Write *no* if the fact is false.

Runner	1st Place	2nd Place	3rd Place	Number
Katie	No			23
Carl	No		No	11
Megan			No	

Step 4 Use the information to answer the other questions. Whenever you write *yes* in a box, you must write *no* in the other boxes.

1. _____ was the runner who had #17, because Carl had #11 and Katie had #23. Write 17 for Megan's number.

2. _____ didn't finish first or third, so he had to finish _____. Write *yes* under 2nd place for Carl, and *no* under 2nd place for Katie and Megan.

3. If Carl finished just behind Megan and he was second, _____ had to be first. Write *yes* under 1st place for Megan.

4. If Katie was not first or second, she had to finish _____.
Write *yes* under 3rd place for Katie.

Step 5 Compare the completed chart to the facts to make sure you are right. After you compare, fill in the list telling who won the blue, red, and yellow ribbons.

Blue Ribbon—First Place _____

Red Ribbon—Second Place _____

Yellow Ribbon—Third Place _____

Practice

1 Shawna, Robert, and Rick baked pies for the school carnival. They made one pie each. Shawna did not bake the peach pie. Robert made a berry pie, but not the strawberry pie. The third pie was made with blueberries. Who made each pie?

Name	Peach	Strawberry	Blueberry
Shawna			
Robert			
Rick			

2 Maylee, Sandra, Kaleel, and Joan are standing in the ticket line. Sandra is last. Joan is not first or third. Kaleel is not first. In what order are they standing? Draw a chart to show your answers.

Short Response Question

3 James, Kathy, Ken, and Michelle are the only students sitting in the fourth row. Neither James nor Michelle is in the first seat. Kathy sits between two boys. In what order are they sitting? Create a drawing to show their seats. Explain how you got your answer.

Lesson 1.3 ▪ Draw pictures, diagrams, and charts to represent problems

> **READY REFERENCE**
> **graph** a drawing used to show information
> **pictograph** a graph that uses pictures to show information

Think About It

Collier's soccer team wants to keep track of the number of practices they have each month. Collier's coach asked him to create a graph of the practices. In June there were 8 practices, in July there were 9 practices, in August there were 5 practices, and in September there were 10 practices. How can Collier use a bar graph to show the information?

Here's How

Step 1 Draw an empty chart that lists the months and numbers that include the highest number of practices in any month.

Month	Number of Practices									
	1	2	3	4	5	6	7	8	9	10
June										
July										
August										
September										

Step 2 Put a mark under the number for each month's practice.

Month	Number of Practices									
	1	2	3	4	5	6	7	8	9	10
June								X		
July									X	
August					X					
September										X

Step 3 Shade in the area from the month to that month's number of practices.

Month	Number of Practices									
	1	2	3	4	5	6	7	8	9	10
June	██████████████████████ (8)									
July	████████████████████████ (9)									
August	██████████████ (5)									
September	██████████████████████████ (10)									

Collier's completed bar graph shows exactly how many practices were held for each month.

🔑 **Practice**

1 Create a bar graph that shows a comparison of the fourth-grade classes at Melissa's school. Mrs. Carson has 28 students, Mr. Jackson has 26 students, and Miss Brown has 30 students.

2 Create a bar graph that compares the favorite foods of students in Sean's class. Eight students chose hamburgers, 12 students chose tacos, and 6 students chose pizza.

3 Create a pictograph for the bar graph in Problem 2. Use drawings of hamburgers, tacos, and pizzas instead of bars.

Hamburgers	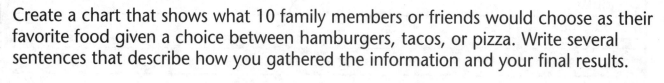
Tacos	
Pizza	

Short Response Question

4 Create a chart that shows what 10 family members or friends would choose as their favorite food given a choice between hamburgers, tacos, or pizza. Write several sentences that describe how you gathered the information and your final results.

_____

_____

_____

Lesson 1.4 ▪ Understand problems by discussing them with classmates

> **READY REFERENCE**
> **interpret** to explain the meaning of

 Think About It

Where do you go to get information? Who do you ask when you aren't sure of something? You might look in a dictionary or an encyclopedia. You might ask your teacher or a parent. Sometimes getting information or sorting out a problem is easiest when you work with one or more classmates.

 Here's How

Your local recycling center wants to know how many people recycle at home and at their place of work. You and your friends want to be able to report to the recycling center. How will you do this?

Step 1 Discuss the problem with a friend. Decide how many other friends you will ask to report along with you. Then decide on the questions that you will ask so you can get the information you need.

Step 2 Invite others to join the project. Make sure each person knows what questions to ask.

Step 3 Collect the information. Make sure that each classmate writes his or her name on the information that he or she collects.

Step 4 As a group, discuss how you want to report the information. You might choose to make a list, a pictograph, or a graph, or write a report. You might choose to report your information in more than one way.

Step 5 Create your report for the recycling center.

By working cooperatively with others, you can find solutions that you might have found difficult if you had worked alone.

 Practice

1 Create a chart that shows the number of brothers and sisters of all the people in your class.

2 Work with a partner to interpret the chart below. Together, write sentences that tell what the chart means.

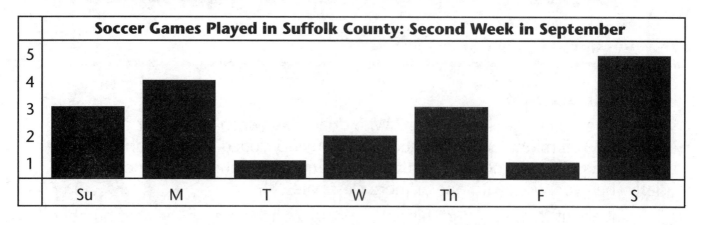

_____

_____

_____

_____

Short Response Question

3 Work with a partner to create a chart on clothing colors. Identify the colors of clothing that your classmates are wearing today. Create the chart for the colors red, blue, green, yellow, purple, and brown. Make a chart for boys' clothes or a chart for girls' clothes. Then write a paragraph that summarizes your data.

_____

_____

_____

_____

Lesson 1.5 ▪ Addition, subtraction, and multiplication in number patterns

> **READY REFERENCE**
> **pattern** a set of symbols that is repeated in a specific order
> **sequence** the order in which numbers are written
> **symbol** a figure that represents, or stands for, something else

 Think About It

What is the next number in the pattern 1, 2, 3, 4, ____? The next number is 5. You can tell that each number is 1 added to the number before it, so the next number is 5. What about 2, 4, 6, ____? This pattern adds 2 each time, so the next number is 8. There are patterns in numbers all around us.

Here's How

One way to recognize number patterns is to create a table, or chart, of the pattern and compare the numbers. The number sequence 1, 3, 6, 10, 15, 21 has a definite pattern. A chart can help you see this pattern.

	1	3	6	10	15	21
pattern ⟶		+2	+3	+4	+5	+6

Using the pattern, what is the next number in the sequence? _____

The next number in the pattern is + 7. So, 21 + 7 = _____

To find number patterns in symbols, you can create the same kind of table to see the pattern.

	◑◑	◪◪	◐◐◑	◪◪◪	◐◐◐◑	◪◪◪◪
pattern ⟶	2	2	3	3	4	4

Another way to make sense of number patterns is to figure out what number a symbol stands for.

● + ● = 6

■ − 3 = ● (Hint: There is only one number which, added to itself equals 6.)

What do the symbols represent?

● = _____   ■ = _____

🔑 Practice

1 What is the next number in this pattern?   5, 6, 8, 9, 11, _____

2 What are the next symbols in this pattern?

☐ * * ● ● ● ☐ ☐ ☐ ☐ * * * * * _____

3 What do the symbols stand for in these number sentences?

● + ● = 4   6 − ● = ◆   ◆ + ● = ■

What number do the symbols represent?

● = _____

◆ = _____

■ = _____

4 Draw the part of the pattern that is missing.

△ △ ☐ ☐ ☐ △ △ ☐ ☐ ☐ _____ ☐ ☐ ☐

5 3 × ▲ = 9

   ▲ = _____

6 ◆ × ■ = 10

   10 − ◆ = 5

   ◆ = _____

   ■ = _____

Short Response Question

7 Create a number problem using symbols. Then solve your number problem. Explain how you got your answer.

_____

_____

_____

Lesson 1.6 ▪ Patterns in sequences of numbers

> **READY REFERENCE**
> **square number** a whole number that is the product of two equal whole numbers
> **triangular number** a number that can be formed into a triangle using dots

 ## Think About It

Karen has 2 trading cards on Tuesday. On Wednesday, she received twice as many trading cards. How many trading cards does she have on Wednesday? If she gets twice as many trading cards on Thursday, how many will she have?

 ## Here's How

You can use counters to find square numbers.

Step 1 Model the items.

1. Place 2 counters on your desk to show the number of trading cards Karen has on Tuesday. Add 2 more counters to show she gets twice as many cards on Wednesday. How many trading cards did Karen have on Wednesday? $2 \times 2 = $ ____. 4 is a square number because it is the product of 2 equal whole numbers. 2 squared $= 4$.

Step 2 Add to the pattern.

2. On Thursday, she got twice as many cards. Use your counters to show how many cards she has on Thursday. She had $4 \times$ ____ $=$ ____ trading cards.

You can use counters to find triangular numbers.

3. Look at these triangular numbers. Complete the pattern for the triangular number 10.

| 1 | 3 | 6 | 10 |

4. Create a table to see the difference in the triangular numbers.

Triangular number →	1	3	6	10
Pattern →		+2	+3	

5. Use the pattern to help you find the next triangular number. The next triangular number is _____.

Practice

Use counters or draw symbols to solve the problems. Write your answers on the lines.

1 Nicholas collected five marbles last week. This week he collected a number that squared the number he had last week. How many marbles did he collect this week?

_____

2 If you square the number 6, what will the new number be? _____

3 The square of 8 is _____.

4 Make a triangular pattern for the number 15 below.

Short Response Question

 5 What is the next number in this triangular number pattern? _____

1

3

6

10

15

On the lines below, explain how you got your answer.

_____

_____

_____

Lesson 1.7 ▪ Symmetry or patterning in number tables

> READY REFERENCE
> **pattern** a set of symbols that is repeated in a specific order

Think About It

Jake and Janet wanted to count to 100 by using different numbers. Jake counted by twos. Janet counted by fives. What kind of pattern would each make on a number table?

Here's How

Fill in Jake's and Janet's counting on a number table.

Jake's Number Table

1	2	3	4	5	6	7	8	9	10
11	12	13	14	15	16	17	18	19	20
21	22	23	24	25	26	27	28	29	30
31	32	33	34	35	36	37	38	39	40
41	42	43	44	45	46	47	48	49	50
51	52	53	54	55	56	57	58	59	60
61	62	63	64	65	66	67	68	69	70
71	72	73	74	75	76	77	78	79	80
81	82	83	84	85	86	87	88	89	90
91	92	93	94	95	96	97	98	99	100

1. Use a red pencil to darken the numbers that Jake says when he counts by twos. Describe how Jake's number table looks.

_____

_____

Janet's Number Table

1	2	3	4	5	6	7	8	9	10
11	12	13	14	15	16	17	18	19	20
21	22	23	24	25	26	27	28	29	30
31	32	33	34	35	36	37	38	39	40
41	42	43	44	45	46	47	48	49	50
51	52	53	54	55	56	57	58	59	60
61	62	63	64	65	66	67	68	69	70
71	72	73	74	75	76	77	78	79	80
81	82	83	84	85	86	87	88	89	90
91	92	93	94	95	96	97	98	99	100

2. Use a blue pencil to darken the numbers that Janet says when she counts by fives. Describe how Janet's number table looks.

_____

_____

🔑 Practice

1 Use a pencil to show the pattern on the number table when you count by tens.

1	2	3	4	5	6	7	8	9	10
11	12	13	14	15	16	17	18	19	20
21	22	23	24	25	26	27	28	29	30
31	32	33	34	35	36	37	38	39	40
41	42	43	44	45	46	47	48	49	50
51	52	53	54	55	56	57	58	59	60
61	62	63	64	65	66	67	68	69	70
71	72	73	74	75	76	77	78	79	80
81	82	83	84	85	86	87	88	89	90
91	92	93	94	95	96	97	98	99	100

2 Use a pencil to show the pattern on the number table when you count by fours.

1	2	3	4	5	6	7	8	9	10
11	12	13	14	15	16	17	18	19	20
21	22	23	24	25	26	27	28	29	30
31	32	33	34	35	36	37	38	39	40
41	42	43	44	45	46	47	48	49	50
51	52	53	54	55	56	57	58	59	60
61	62	63	64	65	66	67	68	69	70
71	72	73	74	75	76	77	78	79	80
81	82	83	84	85	86	87	88	89	90
91	92	93	94	95	96	97	98	99	100

Short Response Question

3 Create your own number table and shade in the numbers when you count by threes. Describe the pattern you have created.

_____

_____

_____

_____

Lesson 1.8 ▪ Money, fractions, and decimals

READY REFERENCE

fraction a number that names a part of a whole

decimal a number with one or more places to the right of a decimal point

decimal point a dot that is used to separate dollars from cents or ones from tenths

---

 Think About It

Carlos has a half-dollar and Maylee has a quarter. They want to write the amount of money they have as a fraction and a decimal. How do they do it?

 Here's How

Each empty square on these grids stands for one penny or 1¢. One hundred squares are equal to 100¢ or one dollar. Beginning at the bottom right of the grid, color in the amount of pennies that Carlos has. Then color in the number of pennies that Maylee has.

Carlos's Money   **Maylee's Money**

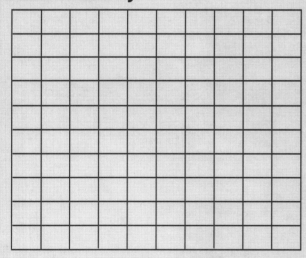   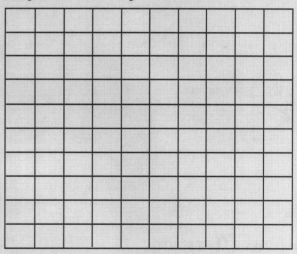

Carlos has _____ ¢ or $\frac{1}{2}$ dollar.   Maylee has _____ ¢ or $\frac{1}{4}$ dollar.

50¢ = $0.50   25¢ = $0.25

Express the amounts as a fraction and a decimal.

$50¢ = \frac{50}{100}$ or $\frac{5}{10} = .5$ $25¢ = \frac{25}{100} = .25$

$\frac{5}{10} = \frac{1}{2}$ $\frac{25}{100} = \frac{1}{4}$

🔑 Practice

For each amount of money shown, write the amount in cents and as a fraction.

1

_____

2

_____

3

_____

4

_____

5

_____

6

_____

7

_____

8

_____

9

_____

Short Response Question

10 On the lines below, write the steps you take to translate four dimes to a decimal. Then explain your steps.

_____

_____

_____

Lesson 1.9 ▪ Verify an answer to a problem

🔑 Think About It

Casey and his brother, Dan, were beginning to collect marbles. They saw some marbles in the window of a game store. Four marbles were lined up left to right in the window display. Casey told his father that he wanted to buy the marble that was the second from the right. Dan thought that marble was the cat's-eye. Casey couldn't remember the marble's name, so Dad tried to help Casey remember the following facts:

1. The names of the four marbles were agate, cat's-eye, swirl, and clear.
2. The clear was between the agate and the cat's-eye.
3. The swirl was the last marble on the right.
4. The agate was not the first on the left.

Was Dan right? Sometimes you can verify, or check, answers by drawing a diagram.

🔑 Here's How

Step 1 Understand. Make sure you read the facts carefully.

Step 2 Plan. Think about how you can solve the problem and verify the answer.

Step 3 Solve.

1. Write the name of the swirl marble on the last marble on the right.

2. The clear was between the agate and the cat's-eye, so it had to be the second from the _____. Write its name where it belongs.

3. Write the name of the agate and the cat's-eye on the correct marble. Look at the drawing to see which marble was second from the right—the cat's-eye.

Step 4 Check and verify. Compare your answer with the facts. Your answer should match each fact in the problem. What was the marble Dan thought Casey wanted? _____ Was Dan's guess the same as the labeled drawing? _____

🔑 Practice

Verify the answer in each of the problems. Follow the steps and show your work.

1 Connie was arranging her sister's model cars. Connie's sister, Anitra, asked Connie to put the purple car at the first of the line. Connie put the red car in front of the blue car. She put the yellow car between the blue car and the red car. She put the purple car next to the red car, but not next to the yellow car. Was the purple car in the front of the line? _____

2 Maria has four photo albums on her shelf. She asked her sister, Carla, to hand her the photo album that was the third from the left. The black album was between the blue album and the yellow album. The blue album is fourth. The other album is red. Carla handed Maria the yellow album. Was that the correct photo album? _____

3 Trung didn't know the age of his cousin Vin. Vin told Trung, "My age is an odd number less than 20 and greater than 10. The sum of the digits is 6." Trung guessed Vin's age as 17. Was Trung correct? _____

Short Response Question

4 On the lines below, explain how you verified the answer for Problem 2.

_____

_____

_____

_____

Lesson 1.10 ▪ Use estimation, number relationships, and mathematical checks

> **READY REFERENCE**
> **estimate** an approximate answer that is close to exact

 Think About It

Michael told his teacher that he had collected about 50 leaves. His number was rounded to the nearest ten. How many leaves could Michael have collected?

 Here's How

Estimates are not exact numbers. When you hear or see the words *about, almost, more than, less than,* or *nearly,* you know that the numbers are probably not exact. The numbers give you a general idea of what the answer is. If Michael's leaf collection is rounded to the nearest ten, how can you estimate how many leaves he has?

1. What numbers would be the nearest to fifty by tens? You can use a number line to help you estimate.

40 41 42 43 44   45 46 47 48 49 50 51 52 53 54   55 56 57 58 59 60

↓   ↓   ↓

| These numbers rounded to the nearest ten are closer to 40. | These numbers rounded to the nearest ten would be 50. | These numbers rounded to the nearest ten are closer to 60. |

2. Michael has between 45 and _____ leaves in his collection. This estimate is not an exact number but can help you determine whether your answer is reasonable or not. Is your answer reasonable? _____

 Practice

1 Nate and Vicki collect action figure trading cards. Nate got 25 cards for his birthday, and Vicki bought almost 70 cards with the money she earned helping Mrs. Brown each afternoon. Vicki's brother gave her 20 cards and Nate traded some marbles for more than 80 cards. How many cards do Nate and Vicki have in their collection?

    A less than 150   **C** exactly 195
    B almost 200   **D** more than 250

2 Which sentence tells how many trading cards Vicki's brother gave her?

    A Vicki's brother gave her less than 20 cards.

    B Vicki's brother gave her almost 20 cards.

    C Vicki's brother gave her exactly 20 cards.

    D Vicki's brother gave her more than 20 cards.

3 Which word in the problem helps you know that "70 cards" is an estimate?

    A earned   **C** bought

    B almost   **D** traded

4 What is the total number of cards in their collection that is exact, not an estimate?

    A 45   **C** 95

    B 90   **D** 105

Short Response Question

5 There are several numbers used in this ad—200, 10, $5, 20, and $3. On the lines below, explain how you can tell which numbers in the ad are estimates and which are exact numbers.

Manuel's Trading Cards

Card Sale on Thursday

More Than 200 New Cards to Choose From

10 Different Action Figure Sets

All Cards Sell for Less Than $5!

Special: First 20 Customers Get a Free Trading Card Worth Over $3!

_____

_____

_____

_____

_____

Lesson 1.11 ▪ Use concrete objects, diagrams, charts, tables, and number lines to solve problems

 Think About It

Abby helped out at the community center every Thursday. The center director, Mr. Garrett, asked Abby to show the third-grade group how to get the right number of paint dishes ready for their art project. There are 4 groups of students. Each group needs 5 different paint dishes. How could Abby show the third graders how many dishes they needed?

Here's How

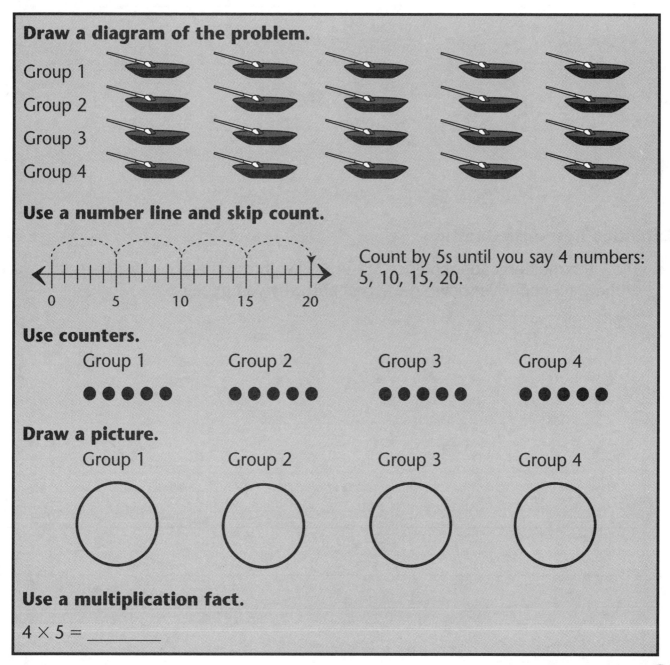

Draw a diagram of the problem.

Group 1

Group 2

Group 3

Group 4

Use a number line and skip count.

Count by 5s until you say 4 numbers: 5, 10, 15, 20.

Use counters.

Group 1   Group 2   Group 3   Group 4
● ● ● ● ●   ● ● ● ● ●   ● ● ● ● ●   ● ● ● ● ●

Draw a picture.

Group 1   Group 2   Group 3   Group 4

Use a multiplication fact.

4 × 5 = _____

 **Practice**

Draw a picture, chart, diagram, table, or number line, or use counters to show each math sentence.

1 $5 + 5$

2 6×5

3 7×3

4 $21 - 11$

5 $20 - 6$

6 6×6

Extended Response Question

7 Show the multiplication sentence 5×7 at least three different ways. Then tell which of the ways you have shown is the best and why you think so.

_____

_____

_____

Lesson 1.12 ▪ Use open sentences, patterns, relationships, and estimation to solve problems

 Think About It

Just as words can be used in sentences, so can numbers. How do you make a number sentence from a word sentence? How do you estimate?

Here's How

Use an open sentence to solve a problem.

1. Jared and his brother Ryan picked apples. Jared picked 35 and Ryan picked 42. How many apples did they pick? What do you know? What do you need to know?

    35 apples + 42 apples = _____ total apples picked

    35 + 42 = _____

2. Coleen and Shanika picked up 25 aluminum cans to take to the recycling center. Kara and Marjie picked up three times as many cans. How many cans did Kara and Marjie pick up?

    25 cans × 3 times as many = _____ cans Marjie and Kara picked up

    25 × 3 = _____

Use estimation to solve a problem. Then use exact numbers to check your estimate.

1. There are 5 fourth-grade classes in your school and about 29 students in each class. Estimate how many fourth-grade students are in your school.

    Round 29 students to 30. Mentally drop the zero and use 3 instead of 30 to make it easy to multiply.

    5 classes × 3 = 15 ◄— Put the zero back = 150

    There are approximately _____ fourth graders.

    Exactly how many fourth graders are there? 5 × 29 = _____

    Compare your estimated and exact answers.

    Estimated _____   Exact _____

Practice

Write a number sentence for each problem. Then solve the number sentence.

1 Joe and Michael want to collect three times as many trading cards as the 72 they already have. How many do they want to collect?

2 Jacinta bought rulers for the 6 students in her cooperative group. The rulers were 38¢ each. How much did she pay?

3 When Jackie was in Grade 2, she climbed 10-foot rocks with her father, who was an experienced climber. In Grade 4, she can climb twice as high. If she can climb twice as high again in Grade 6, how high will she be able to climb?

4 Tanya has a CD case that holds 160 CDs. There are four sections in the CD case. Each section holds the same number of CDs. How many CDs are in each section?

Short Response Question

5 The state of New York uses an average of 583 gallons of water per person every day. The smallest town in the state is Dering Harbor, with a population of 28 people. How many gallons of water are used in Dering Harbor for one day?

Part A Write a number sentence, and then solve it.

Part B On the lines below, tell how you would calculate the water usage in Dering Harbor for a week, a month, and a year.

_____

_____

_____

Lesson 1.13 • Identify missing information in a story problem

🔑 Think About It

To solve a mystery, you must have all the facts. To solve a math problem, you must have all the facts. How do you know whether or not you have all the facts?

🔑 Here's How

Read a story problem carefully. Once you have read the problem, create a picture in your mind. List the facts. Then write the question you want to answer. Look at the facts and the question. Is anything missing? Can you write a number sentence?

Leticia and her mother went to the laundromat to wash and dry their clothes. The dryers cost 25¢ for ten minutes. Their clothes took 40 minutes to dry. How much did they spend to dry their clothes?

1. List the facts: Dryers cost 25¢ for 10 minutes.
   Drying took 40 minutes.
   They needed 4 ten-minute drying periods.

2. Write the question. How much did the dryer cost for 40 minutes?

3. Is anything missing? _____

4. Can you write a number sentence? $40 \div 10 =$ _____

   _____ $\times 25¢ =$ _____

Jamal walks 6 blocks from home to school every day. It takes him 10 minutes to walk from home to school. Will he make it to school by 8:30?

1. List the facts: Jamal walks 6 blocks.

   It takes him 10 minutes to walk 6 blocks.

2. Write the question. What time will Jamal get to school?

3. Is anything missing? _____

4. Can you write a number sentence? _____

 **Practice**

Read the problems and answer the questions.

1 Liz wanted to call her mom from a public telephone. She has 2 quarters and 2 dimes. Does she have enough money for the call? What information is missing?

   A The distance from home
   B The cost of the call
   C The time of day
   D No information is missing

2 Carla took 20 coupons with her to the video arcade. Each arcade game cost 4 coupons. Did Carla have enough coupons for 5 games? What information is missing?

   F How long Carla wanted to play
   G How far away she lived from the arcade
   H How many coupons it took for each game
   J No information is missing

3 Nathan and his grandpa are going to a movie on Saturday. Special student prices are $2 every Saturday. How much will they spend? What information is missing?

   A The number of people going
   B The price of Nathan's ticket
   C The price of his grandpa's ticket
   D No information is missing

4 José wants to ride his bike to his friend Jack's house. It takes him 20 minutes to ride the 3-mile trip. Can he arrive at Jack's by 3:00 in the afternoon? What information is missing?

   F The distance between houses
   G The time José left his house
   H The number of blocks
   J No information is missing

Short Response Question

5 Write a problem with missing information. Then rewrite the problem with the needed information and solve the problem.

_____

_____

_____

_____

Directions
Use a separate piece of paper to show your work.

1 What does this array not show?

A $4 \times 5 = 20$
B $5 + 5 + 5 + 5 + 5 = 20$
C $5 \times 4 = 20$
D $4 + 4 + 4 + 4 + 4 = 20$

2 What does this bar graph show?

Our Class's Favorite Foods

Hamburger	
Tacos	
Pizza	

1 2 3 4 5 6 7 8

F The class likes tacos better than pizza.

G The class likes hamburgers as much as tacos.

H The class likes pizza better than tacos or hamburgers.

J More students like tacos and hamburgers than pizza.

3 Karen, Mike, Jaleel, and Maria are in line. Maria is standing between Karen and Mike. Jaleel is the last person in line. Karen is not the first person. List the order in which they are in line. Draw a picture to show your answer.

4 Carlos and Mack want to buy some new trading cards. They already have 15. They want three times as many cards. How many will they have? Write a number sentence and solve the problem.

Answer _____

5 Draw in the next three symbols in this pattern.

● ■ ● ● ■ ■ ● ● ● ___ ___ ___

6 Carmen has $12.00 to buy stamps for her collection. She wants to buy the new stamps that have action figures on them. She thinks she can get at least 20 stamps for her collection. Can Carmen get the stamps she wants? What information is missing?

A How many stamps she wants
B The kind of stamps she wants
C How much each stamp costs
D No information is missing

7 Draw a picture, chart, diagram, table, or number line to show the math sentence $20 - 6$.

Lesson 2.1 ▪ Whole numbers to hundred millions

> **READY REFERENCE**
> **digit** a symbol used to write whole numbers (0, 1, 2, 3, 4, 5, 6, 7, 8, and 9)

🔑 Think About It

Whole numbers can be written in standard form, word form, short word form, or expanded form. Can you write the digits 325185231 in four different forms?

🔑 Here's How

Standard form Large numbers are grouped in threes, using commas, beginning at the right of the number. 325185231 is written as 325,185,231.

Word form three hundred twenty-five million, one hundred eighty-five thousand, two hundred thirty-one

Short word form 325 million, 185 thousand, 2 hundred 31

Expanded form 300,000,000 + 20,000,000 + 5,000,000 + 100,000 + 80,000 + 5,000 + 200 + 30 + 1

🔑 Practice

Write each number in its expanded form.

1 2,498 _____

_____

2 35,689 _____

_____

3 451,309 _____

_____

4 2,342,179 _____

_____

5 32,498,352 _____

_____

6 672,387,143 _____

_____

Add commas to the following numbers.

7 3990 _____   **8** 321845 _____   **9** 58990421_____

Write the number in word form in A and then in short word form in B.

10 287,369,435   **A** _____

_____

B _____

Short Response Question

11 Pam's mom traveled twenty-eight thousand, six hundred thirty-one miles last year for her job. Write the number of miles she traveled in standard form. _____

Short word form: _____

Expanded form: _____

Which form should she use in a letter to her cousins? Explain why.

_____

_____

Lesson 2.2 ▪ Use ordinal numbers through 500th

> **READY REFERENCE**
> **ordinal number** a number that shows order or position

 Think About It

Your class wants to enter a national spelling bee. There are 499 entries already. What will be your entry position?

 Here's How

Ordinal numbers and their word names follow a pattern, no matter how large the number is. For example, 22nd is written as twenty-second and 322nd is written as three hundred twenty-second.

Ordinal numbers		Ordinal word names	
1st	9th	first	ninth
2nd	10th	second	tenth
3rd	11th	third	eleventh
4th	21st	fourth	twenty-first
5th	22nd	fifth	twenty-second
6th	23rd	sixth	twenty-third
7th	100th	seventh	one hundredth
8th	105th	eighth	one hundred fifth

Your class will bring the total entries in the spelling bee to 500. Your entry position will be 500th or five hundredth.

 Practice

Write the ordinal word name.

1 45th _____

2 19th _____

3 62nd _____

4 403rd _____

5 381st _____

6 299th _____

Write the ordinal number.

7 fifty-fifth _____

8 ninety-second _____

9 eighty-third _____

10 forty-first _____

11 one hundred fourth _____

12 two hundred fifty-ninth _____

Solve the following problems.

13 Beth is waiting in line for a movie. There are 39 people in front of her. What is her place in line?

_____

14 Leon's grandfather is 79 years old. What is the ordinal number for his next birthday?

_____

15 John's audition number is 72. Eric's number is the next one. What is Eric's position in the audition?

_____

16 Alejandro's birthday is on September 12. His cousin's birthday is 9 days later. What is the ordinal number for his cousin's birthday?

_____

Write the ordinal numbers that are 9 more and 11 less for each number.

17 98 _____

18 141 _____

_____

_____

Short Response Question

19 Write the ordinal number and the ordinal word name for each of the following.

A The number of the last day of the year _____

B The last day of September _____

C The number of the last month of the year _____

D The next to the last week of the year _____

Lesson 2.3 ▪ Fractions, decimals, money, and metrics

> **READY REFERENCE**
> **fraction** a number that names part of a whole
> **decimal** a number with one or more places to the right of the decimal point

🔑 Think About It

Fractions or decimals can be used when dealing with money or metric measurements. For example, 100 cents are in one dollar. How many cents are in $\frac{1}{4}$ dollar? How would you write this amount using a decimal?

🔑 Here's How

Fractions or decimals and money.

Step 1 How many cents are in $\frac{1}{4}$ dollar? Divide 100 cents by 4.

There are _____ cents in $\frac{1}{4}$ dollar.

Step 2 Twenty-five cents, or $\frac{1}{4}$ dollar, can be written as $0.25.

Fractions or decimals and metric measurements.

Step 1 How many centimeters are in $\frac{1}{4}$ meter? Divide 100 centimeters by 4.

There are _____ centimeters in $\frac{1}{4}$ meter.

Step 2 Twenty-five cm, or $\frac{1}{4}$ m, can be written as 0.25m.

🔑 Practice

Write as a decimal.

1 35 cents $_____

2 82 cents $_____

3 18 cents $_____

4 98 cents $_____

5 56 cents $_____

6 75 cents $_____

Fill in the blanks for each problem.

7 $\frac{1}{2}$ dollar = _____ cents or $_____

8 $\frac{3}{4}$ dollar = _____ cents or $_____

9 $\frac{1}{10}$ dollar = _____ cents or $_____

10 $\frac{1}{20}$ dollar = _____ cents or $_____

Write as a decimal.

11 53 cm = _____ m   **12** 38 cm = _____ m   **13** 15 cm = _____ m

14 89 cm = _____ m   **15** 67 cm = _____ m   **16** 75 cm = _____ m

Write the problem in numbers and find the answer.

17 $\frac{1}{2}$ meter = _____ cm or _____ m   **18** $\frac{3}{4}$ meter = _____ cm or _____ m

19 $\frac{1}{10}$ meter = _____ cm or _____ m   **20** $\frac{1}{20}$ meter = _____ cm or _____ m

21 Jemma thinks her collection of baseball cards is worth $10.50. She tells Marta she will sell $\frac{1}{2}$ of her collection for $\frac{1}{2}$ of the cost. How much will Marta pay? Show your work.

22 Vince earned $20.00 by washing cars and cutting lawns. He wants to put $\frac{1}{4}$ of the money into his savings account. How much will he save? Show your work.

Short Response Question

23 Sue paid $\frac{1}{2}$ dollar for $\frac{1}{2}$ meter of lace trim. She paid $_____ for _____ m of trim. Compare the two numbers. Show your work and explain how you got your answer.

_____

_____

_____

Lesson 2.4 ▪ Fractions and decimals in daily life

 Think About It

How do you use fractions and decimals in your life? Many recipes use fractions. Fractions and decimals are often used in giving directions and in measuring distances. We use decimals every time we use money.

Here's How

Double a recipe.

Michael wants to double a recipe. He has to multiply each ingredient by 2 or add the ingredients twice.

Ingredients: $\frac{1}{2}$ cup flour, $\frac{3}{4}$ cup sugar, $1\frac{1}{4}$ cup shortening

1. $\frac{1}{2} \times 2 = \frac{2}{2}$, so Michael needs _____ c flour.

2. $\frac{3}{4} \times 2 = \frac{6}{4}$, so Michael needs _____ c sugar.

3. $1\frac{1}{4} + 1\frac{1}{4} = 2\frac{2}{4}$, so Michael needs _____ c shortening.

Give directions or measure distances.

Jimmy's mom needs directions to Joseph's house. Jimmy tells his mom to travel .25 miles north from their house and turn right. How would you write the distance as a fraction?

$.25 = \frac{25}{100} =$ _____ mile

Use decimals to count money.

How much money does Sara have if she has 1 quarter, 1 dime, and 1 nickel?

1. Write each coin as a decimal: 1 quarter = .25, 1 dime = _____ , 1 nickel = _____

2. Add the decimals: \$0.25 + \$0.10 + \$0.05 = _____

Practice

Write each fraction as a decimal.

1. Ed walks $1\frac{1}{4}$ miles to school every day. He walks _____ miles to school.

2. The post office is $\frac{1}{2}$ mile past the grocery store. The post office is _____ miles from the grocery store.

3   Sue has 3 quarters. Sue has $_____.

4   Bob's best friend gave him $2\frac{1}{2}$ dollars or $_____.

Fill in the blanks.

5   Jill's recipe for pie crust makes enough for one pie. She wants to make three pies. How much of each ingredient will she need? Show your work.

One pie	**Three pies**
$1\frac{1}{3}$ c flour	_____ c flour
$\frac{1}{2}$ c shortening	_____ c shortening
$\frac{1}{8}$ c sugar	_____ c sugar
3 T water	_____ T water

Extended Response Question

6   Jason has 3 quarters, 4 dimes, and 2 nickels. He wants to donate $1.00 to a school fund. Which coins could he use for the donation? Show your work and explain your answer.

_____

_____

_____

Lesson 2.5 · Using manipulatives to model number relationships

READY REFERENCE
place value the value of a digit based on its position in a number

 Think About It

Look at the number 1,111. Each digit has a place value. It tells how many thousands or hundreds or tens there are. Look at the number 1.11. Each digit has a place value. It tells how many ones or tenths or hundredths there are. Base-10 blocks and grid paper can help you understand place values.

 Here's How

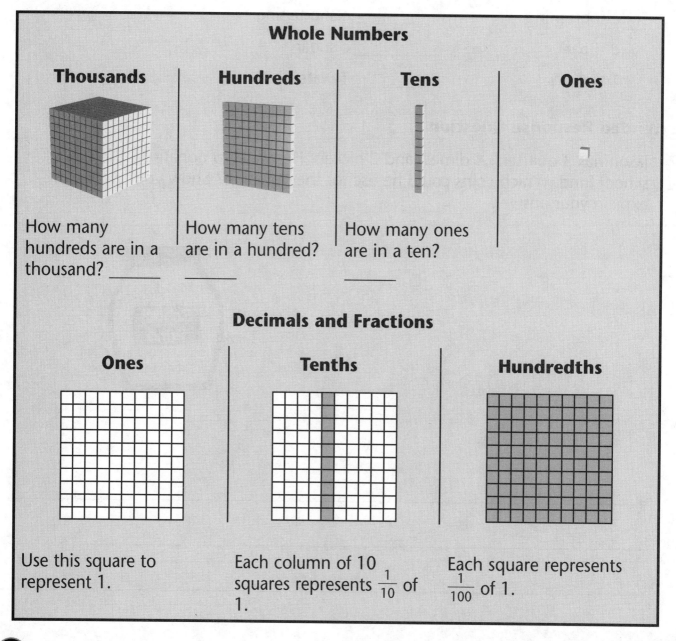

Whole Numbers

Thousands	Hundreds	Tens	Ones
How many hundreds are in a thousand? _____	How many tens are in a hundred? _____	How many ones are in a ten? _____	

Decimals and Fractions

Ones	Tenths	Hundredths
Use this square to represent 1.	Each column of 10 squares represents $\frac{1}{10}$ of 1.	Each square represents $\frac{1}{100}$ of 1.

🔑 Practice

In A, write the number in expanded form. In B, write the number in standard form.

1

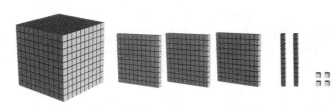

A _____

B _____

2

A _____

B _____

Write the number as a mixed number in A and as a decimal in B.

3

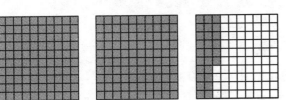

A _____

B _____

Short Response Question

4 Write the numbers represented by the pictures in Part A and Part B.

Part A

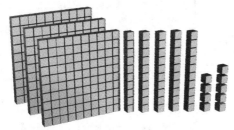

Answer _____

Part B

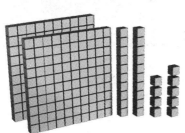

Answer _____

Lesson 2.6 ▪ Manipulatives and odd and even numbers

> **READY REFERENCE**
> **even number** a number, such as 2, 4, and 6, that is divisible by 2
> **odd number** a number, such as 1, 3, and 5, that is not divisible by 2

  Think About It

How can you use counters to predict whether the answer to an addition, subtraction, or multiplication problem will be an odd or even number? Use counters in *Here's How* to write problems and find out.

Here's How

Adding odd and even numbers.

1. *Two even numbers.* Write a problem. _____
   When you add two even numbers, the sum is _____.

2. *Two odd numbers.* Write a problem. _____
   When you add two odd numbers, the sum is _____.

3. *One even and one odd number.* Write a problem. _____
   When you add an even and an odd number, the sum is _____.

Subtracting odd and even numbers.

1. *Two even numbers.* Write a problem. _____
   When you subtract even numbers, the difference is _____.

2. *Two odd numbers.* Write a problem. _____
   When you subtract odd numbers, the difference is _____.

3. *An even number minus an odd number.* Write a problem. _____
   When you subtract an odd number from an even number, the difference is _____.

4. *An odd number minus an even number.* Write a problem. _____
   When you subtract an even number from an odd number, the difference is _____.

Multiplying odd and even numbers.
Use your counters to make up problems.

1. *Two even numbers.* Write a problem. _____
   When you multiply two even numbers, the product is _____.

2. *Two odd numbers.* Write a problem. _____
   When you multiply two odd numbers, the product is _____.

3. *One even and one odd number.* Write a problem. _____ When
   you multiply an even and an odd number, the product is _____.

 Practice

Use counters for Problems 1–4.

1 Kendra has 33 cookies and James has 48 cookies. Are there an even or odd number of cookies in all?

_____

2 Fifteen people in Ann's classroom have 6 people in their families. Is the total number of people odd or even?

_____

 3 Adam has 5 apples and gave 3 apples to Jan. Does Adam have an even or odd number of apples left?

_____

4 Five apple pies have each been cut into 5 pieces. Is there an odd or even number of pieces of pie?

_____

Short Response Question

5 Which one of these bags has an even number of beads? Circle the letter.

A  30 **B**  41 **C**  23 **D**  13

Explain how you know it is an even number.

_____

_____

Lesson 2.7 ▪ Prime numbers

> **READY REFERENCE**
> **prime number** a number that has only two factors, itself and 1
> **composite number** a whole number greater than 1 with more than two factors

⚏ Think About It

The number 1 does not have 2 factors, so it is not a prime number. What are the prime numbers between 2 and 50?

⚏ Here's How

Use the chart below to find the prime numbers between 2 and 50.

1	2	3	4	5	6	7	8	9	10
11	12	13	14	15	16	17	18	19	20
21	22	23	24	25	26	27	28	29	30
31	32	33	34	35	36	37	38	39	40
41	42	43	44	45	46	47	48	49	50

Step 1 Cross off the number 1. It has only one factor, so it is not a prime number.

Step 2 Circle the number 2. The number 2 has two factors (2 × 1), so 2 is a prime number. Starting with 4, cross off each multiple of 2.

Step 3 Circle the number 3. Cross off each multiple of 3 that has not already been crossed off.

Step 4 Repeat the process in Step 3 for the numbers 5 and 7.

Step 5 Circle the numbers that haven't been crossed off. These are the prime numbers from 1 to 50. The numbers that were crossed off are the composite numbers up to 50, except for 1.

Write the prime numbers between 2 and 50. _____

_____

🔑 Practice

1 _____ is a prime number between 32 and 40.

   A 31   **B** 39   **C** 37   **D** 23

2 _____ is a prime number between 21 and 30.

   A 23   **B** 25   **C** 40   **D** 24

Complete the following number sentences using prime numbers.

3 ___ + ___ = 18   **4** ___ + ___ = 12   **5** ___ + ___ = 36

6 ___ + ___ = 24   **7** ___ + ___ = 45   **8** ___ + ___ = 50

9 ___ + ___ = 22   **10** ___ + ___ = 20

Complete the following number sentences with a prime number and a composite number.

11 ___ × ___ = 18   **12** ___ × ___ = 40   **13** ___ × ___ = 45

Short Response Question

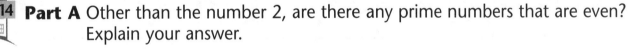

14 **Part A** Other than the number 2, are there any prime numbers that are even? Explain your answer.

_____

_____

    Part B Can any prime number be divided evenly between two people? Explain your answer.

_____

_____

_____

Lesson 2.8 ▪ Skip counting

🔑 Think About It

Skipping to every fifth number is called counting by 5s or skip counting. Skipping to every tenth number is called counting by 10s or skip counting. Skip counting can make it easier to multiply numbers.

🔑 Here's How

Nickels and dimes can be used to practice skip counting by 5s and 10s.

1. How many nickels are pictured above? _____

2. Count the nickels using skip counting. 5, 10, ____ , 20, ____ , ____ , 35, ____ , ____ , ____ , 55, ____

3. How much are the nickels worth? 12 × 5¢ = 60¢

4. How many dimes are pictured? _____

5. How much are the dimes worth? 6 × 10¢ = 60¢

6. Count the dimes using skip counting. 10, ____ , 30, 40, ____ , ____

7. Was it faster to count to 60 by 5s or by 10s? _____

🔑 Practice

Use skip counting to find the products.

1 3 × 2,000 = _____ 2,000, 4,000, _____

2 5 × 200 = _____ _____

3 10 × 8 = _____ _____

4 100 × 5 = _____ _____

Use counters to skip count.

5 $2 \times 6 =$ ____

6 $3 \times 4 =$ ____

7 $5 \times 2 =$ ____

8 $5 \times 3 =$ ____

9 $13 \times 5 =$ ____

10 $15 \times 10 =$ ____

11 $13 \times 2 =$ ____

12 $17 \times 5 =$ ____

13 Julia has a collection of dimes and nickels. She has 15 nickels and 9 dimes. How much money does she have? Use skip counting to find the answer. Show your work.

_____

Short Response Question

14 Damon has 6 nickels and 6 dimes. If he gives 3 nickels and 3 dimes to his sister, how much will each of them have? Use skip counting in solving the problem. Show your work and explain your answer.

_____

_____

_____

Lesson 2.9 ▪ Numerators and denominators

> **READY REFERENCE**
> **numerator** names the number of equal parts represented
> **denominator** names the total number of equal parts

Think About It

Keshawn's mom baked an apple pie, a cherry pie, and a blueberry pie for a family reunion. Six people want apple pie, 4 people want cherry pie, and 3 people want blueberry pie. She wants to divide each pie equally between the people who want each kind. If one person has taken a slice of each pie, what fraction is used to represent that one piece?

Here's How

The apple pie is divided into _____ equal pieces. 6 is the denominator because 6 = the total number of equal parts of the pie. _____ slice of the pie is gone. 1 is the numerator because 1 out of 6 pieces is gone.

$\frac{1}{6}$ of the pie is gone. $\frac{1}{6}$ ← numerator
← denominator

The cherry pie is divided into _____ equal pieces. _____ is missing.

numerator → ___ of the cherry pie is gone.
denominator →

Write the fraction that represents the missing part of blueberry pie. _____

Practice

Write the fraction for the shaded parts of each figure.

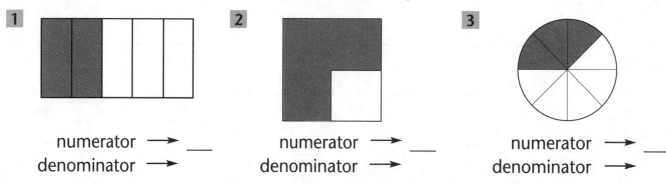

1 numerator → ___
   denominator → ___

2 numerator → ___
   denominator → ___

3 numerator → ___
   denominator → ___

Name the numerator and the denominator for each fraction.

4 $\frac{5}{6}$ numerator ____   **5** $\frac{1}{4}$ numerator ____   **6** $\frac{9}{21}$ numerator ____

denominator ____   denominator ____   denominator ____

Draw a figure to represent each fraction.

7 $\frac{2}{3}$ **8** $\frac{4}{4}$ **9** $\frac{1}{6}$

10 A cake is cut into 12 equal pieces. Three sisters take 2 pieces each. What fraction of the cake did the three sisters take? Write the fraction. Shade the cake to show the pieces taken by the sisters.

 11 Use your pattern blocks. How many triangles would it take to cover $\frac{1}{2}$ of this shape? ____

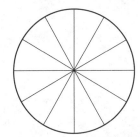

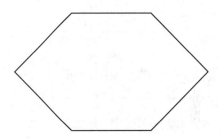

Short Response Question

 12

Nicole's pie is cut into 3 pieces. Can the fraction $\frac{2}{3}$ be used to describe the shaded pieces? Explain your answer.

_____

_____

_____

Lesson 2.10 ▪ Order fractions and decimals

 Think About It

How would you order these fractions and decimals from least to greatest?

.7 $\qquad$ $\frac{2}{5}$ $\qquad$ $\frac{1}{2}$

 Here's How

Use fraction pieces.

Step 1 Change the decimal to a fraction. $.7 = \frac{7}{10}$

Step 2 Use fraction pieces to compare the fractions.

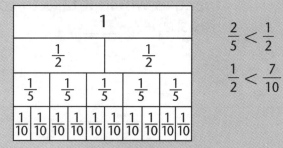

$\frac{2}{5} < \frac{1}{2}$

$\frac{1}{2} < \frac{7}{10}$

Step 3 Write the numbers in order from least to greatest: $\frac{2}{5}, \frac{1}{2}, .7$

Find the common denominator.

Step 1 Find the common denominator to compare the fractions and the decimal.

1. Rewrite the decimal as an equivalent fraction. $.7 = \text{—}$

2. What is the denominator? _____

3. Rewrite the fractions using the common denominator.

$\frac{7}{10}$ $\qquad$ $\frac{2}{5} = \frac{}{10}$ $\qquad$ $\frac{1}{2} = \frac{}{10}$

Step 2 Compare the numerators.

$\frac{4}{10} < \frac{5}{10}$ $\qquad$ $\frac{5}{10} < \frac{7}{10}$

Step 3 Write the numbers in order from least to greatest. _____

🔑 Practice

Compare each pair of numbers using <, >, or =.

1 $\frac{4}{5}$ ____ $\frac{2}{5}$

2 $\frac{1}{2}$ ____ $\frac{4}{8}$

3 $\frac{5}{12}$ ____ $\frac{11}{24}$

4 .4 ____ $\frac{1}{2}$

5 .78 ____ .79

6 .9 ____ .92

Write the numbers in order from greatest to least.

7 $\frac{1}{2}$ $\frac{1}{4}$ $\frac{1}{3}$ _____

8 $\frac{4}{10}$ .6 $\frac{4}{5}$ .2   _____

9 Look at the batting averages for the school softball team. The highest average wins the batting title. List how the batters finished from the lowest to highest average.

____ Sammy .456   ____ Leetha .459   ____ Paul .432   ___ Eduardo .448

_____

10 Recipe 1 calls for $\frac{3}{4}$ t cinnamon and Recipe 2 calls for $\frac{5}{8}$ t cinnamon. Which recipe uses the most cinnamon? Show your work.

_____

Short Response Question

11 Use fraction pieces to order each set from greatest to least.
Explain your work using < and >.

Part A $\frac{2}{3}, \frac{5}{6}, \frac{1}{4}$ **Part B** $\frac{1}{2}, \frac{5}{8}, \frac{3}{4}$

_____   _____

_____   _____

Part C .6, $\frac{7}{8}, \frac{1}{3}$

_____

1									
$\frac{1}{2}$									
$\frac{1}{3}$									
$\frac{1}{4}$									
$\frac{1}{6}$									
$\frac{1}{8}$									
$\frac{1}{10}$									

Lesson 2.11 ▪ Equivalent fractions

> **READY REFERENCE**
> **equivalent fractions** fractions that name the same amount

 Think About It

How do you find an equivalent fraction for $\frac{3}{4}$?

 Here's How

Use fraction pieces.

Step 1 Place 3 of the $\frac{1}{4}$ fraction pieces in a line.

Step 2 Place $\frac{1}{8}$ pieces next to the three $\frac{1}{4}$ pieces. How many $\frac{1}{8}$ pieces does it take to equal $\frac{3}{4}$? _____

So, $\frac{}{8} = \frac{3}{4}$. Shade all the sections that equal $\frac{3}{4}$.

How many $\frac{1}{16}$s equal $\frac{3}{4}$? _____

1			
$\frac{1}{2}$		$\frac{1}{2}$	
$\frac{1}{4}$	$\frac{1}{4}$	$\frac{1}{4}$	$\frac{1}{4}$
$\frac{1}{8}$ $\frac{1}{8}$	$\frac{1}{8}$ $\frac{1}{8}$	$\frac{1}{8}$ $\frac{1}{8}$	$\frac{1}{8}$ $\frac{1}{8}$
$\frac{1}{16}$ ...	...	...	...

Multiply the numerator and denominator by the same number.

Step 1 Write the problem. $\frac{3}{4} = \frac{?}{12}$

Step 2 Look at the denominators. $\frac{3}{4} = \frac{?}{12}$ $4 \times ? = 12$

Step 3 Multiply the numerator by 3. $\frac{3}{4} \times \frac{3}{3} = \frac{9}{12}$

$\frac{3}{4} = \frac{9}{12}$, so $\frac{3}{4}$ and $\frac{9}{12}$ are equivalent fractions.

 Practice

1 Look at the picture in *Here's How*. Name fractions that are equivalent to $\frac{1}{2}$.

_____

Find a set of equivalent fractions for each picture.

2

1		
$\frac{1}{3}$	$\frac{1}{3}$	$\frac{1}{3}$

$\frac{1}{6}$	$\frac{1}{6}$	$\frac{1}{6}$	$\frac{1}{6}$	$\frac{1}{6}$	$\frac{1}{6}$

$1 = \frac{3}{3} = \frac{6}{6}$

3

1	
$\frac{1}{2}$	$\frac{1}{2}$

$\frac{1}{4}$	$\frac{1}{4}$	$\frac{1}{4}$	$\frac{1}{4}$

$1 = \frac{2}{2} = \frac{4}{4}$

4

1				
$\frac{1}{5}$	$\frac{1}{5}$	$\frac{1}{5}$	$\frac{1}{5}$	$\frac{1}{5}$

$\frac{1}{10}$	$\frac{1}{10}$	$\frac{1}{10}$	$\frac{1}{10}$	$\frac{1}{10}$	$\frac{1}{10}$	$\frac{1}{10}$	$\frac{1}{10}$	$\frac{1}{10}$	$\frac{1}{10}$

$1 = \frac{5}{5} = \frac{10}{10}$

Fill in the missing numbers to form equivalent fractions.

5 $\frac{4 \times 2}{6 \times 2} = \frac{8}{12}$

6 $\frac{1 \times 3}{3 \times 3} = \frac{3}{9}$

7 $\frac{2 \times 4}{3 \times 4} = \frac{8}{12}$

8 $\frac{1 \times 4}{5 \times 4} = \frac{4}{20}$

9 $\frac{5 \times 3}{8 \times 3} = \frac{15}{24}$

10 $\frac{1 \times 6}{2 \times 6} = \frac{6}{12}$

11 $\frac{1 \times 5}{4 \times 5} = \frac{5}{20}$

12 $\frac{3 \times 2}{4 \times 2} = \frac{6}{8}$

Find equivalent fractions for the following.

13 $\frac{3}{8} = \frac{9}{24}$

14 $\frac{4}{5} = \frac{8}{20}$ — $\frac{16}{}$

15 $\frac{8}{9} = \frac{64}{72}$

16 $\frac{2}{5} = \frac{4}{10}$

17 Kevin and Missy each ordered pizzas. Kevin's pizza is cut into 12 pieces and Missy's pizza is cut into 8 pieces. What fraction of each pizza would have to be eaten for $\frac{1}{2}$ of each pizza to be left?

A $\frac{5}{12}$ and $\frac{4}{8}$

B $\frac{6}{12}$ and $\frac{4}{8}$

C $\frac{2}{12}$ and $\frac{2}{8}$

D $\frac{12}{2}$ and $\frac{8}{2}$

Short Response Question

18 Paul and Rita are each working on puzzles with the same number of pieces. Paul's puzzle is $\frac{2}{5}$ finished. Rita's puzzle is $\frac{1}{3}$ finished. Have they finished the same amount of their puzzles? Explain your answer. Show your work.

_____

_____

Lesson 2.12 ▪ Number lines and coordinates

> **READY REFERENCE**
> **negative integer** a whole number less than zero
> **ordered pair** a pair of numbers that describe the location of a point on a grid

 Think About It

How would the following numbers be placed on a number line?

$$-4 \qquad\qquad 4 \qquad\qquad \frac{1}{4}$$

 Here's How

Use number lines.

Step 1 Look at the number line. Count over to 4.

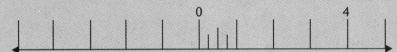

Step 2 Count from the 0 to write the numbers on the line.

1. ⁻4 is a negative integer, so we know that it is less than 0. What whole number can you add to ⁻4 to equal 0? _____ Write ⁻4 on the number line.

2. $\frac{1}{4}$ is a fraction. The space between 0 and 1 is divided into 4 equal parts. Write $\frac{1}{4}$ on the number line.

3. Write $\frac{1}{4}$, ⁻4, and 4 in order from least to greatest. _____

Find a point on a grid with ordered pairs.

Step 1 Put your pencil at 0. Move right 4 units. This is the first number in the ordered pair.

Step 2 Now move up 2 units and label a point (•). This is the second number in the ordered pair. The ordered pair is (4, 2).

Step 3 Repeat the steps for the ordered pair (⁻4, ⁻2). First, move left 4 units to ⁻4. Next, will you move up 2 units or down 2 units? _____ How do you know?

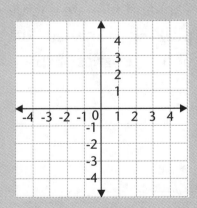

🔑 Practice

Place the fractions on the number lines.

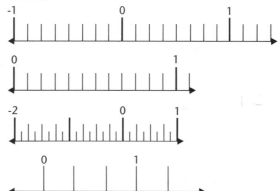

1 $\frac{3}{4}, \frac{1}{4}$

2 $\frac{1}{12}, \frac{5}{12}, \frac{10}{12}$

3 $-\frac{5}{8}, \frac{5}{8}, \frac{7}{8}$

4 $\frac{1}{3}$

Circle the correct letter.

5 On a number line, the fraction $-\frac{9}{10}$ will be

   A to the right of 0   **B** to the left of 0   **C** above the 0   **D** close to 1

6 On number lines, all negative numbers are found

   F to the right of 0   **G** to the left of 0   **H** below the line **J** in the center

Short Response Question

7 Use the grid to plot a point for the following ordered pairs: (2, 3), (-2, 3), (-2, -3), (2, -3). Connect the points in order and connect the last to the first and describe what you see.

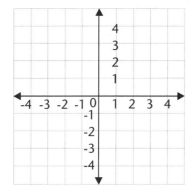

_____

_____

Lesson 2.13 ▪ Place value for millions and hundredths

> **READY REFERENCE**
> **place value** the value of a digit based on its position in a number

🔑 Think About It

How do you read the number 25,341,582.21?

🔑 Here's How

Use a place value chart.

Each digit has a place value. It tells how many millions, thousands, hundreds, tens, ones, tenths, or hundredths there are. Moving to the left of the decimal point, each group of three digits is called a period. Each period has ones, tens, and hundreds. The value of a digit is shown by its place in the number. For example, the value of 3 in this number is 300,000.

MILLIONS			THOUSANDS			ONES				
hundred millions	ten millions	one millions	hundred thousands	ten thousands	one thousands	hundreds	tens	ones	tenths	hundredths
2	5,	3	4	1,	5	8	2	.	2	1

The expanded form of the number shows place value. 25,341,582.21 = 20,000,000 + 5,000,000 + 300,000 + 40,000 + 1,000 + 500 + 80 + 2 + .2 + .01

25,341,582.21 can be written as 20 million + ___ million + 300 thousand + ___ thousand + ___ thousand + 5 hundred + ___ tens + ___ ones + 2 tenths + ___ hundredth.

Read the number as twenty-five million, three hundred forty-one thousand, five hundred eighty-two and twenty-one hundredths. The decimal point is read *as and*.

🔑 Practice

Write the following number in expanded form and word form.

1 2,683,337.01   Expanded form: _____

_____

_____

Word form: _____

_____

_____

Place commas in the numbers.

2 2 5 3 2 1 0 6 . 0 5   **3** 8 9 1 0 0 2 7 0 . 5   **4** 9 0 0 4 0 1 6 9 0 . 3 3

What is the value of the digit 3 in each number?

5 83,458,001.91   **6** 5,248,010.13

A 300,000   **C** 3,000,000   **F** .03   **H** 3

B .03   **D** 3,000   **G** 30   **J** 300

Write the following number in standard form.

7 Fifteen million, two hundred fifteen thousand, three hundred fifteen and fifteen hundredths _____

Short Response Question

8 Draw a place value chart and place 89,023,157.06 on the chart.

Write the word form of the number. _____

_____

_____

Lesson 2.14 ▪ Whole numbers to millions

> **READY REFERENCE**
> **compare** examine two or more numbers to see which is greater or lesser
> **order** put three or more numbers in order from greatest to least or from least to greatest
> < less than
> > greater than

 Think About It

Malik, Tim, Lily, and Carmen compared their scores on a video game. Malik has 7,500,100 points, Tim has 750,500, Lily has 75,500, and Carmen has 750,509. How do you order these points from the greatest number to the least number?

 Here's How

Step 1 Line up the numbers by the ones column.
The number with the most digits is greatest.
The number with the fewest digits is least.

$$7,500,100$$
$$750,500$$
$$75,500$$
$$750,509$$

1. Which number has the most digits? _____

2. Which number has the fewest digits? _____

Step 2 Compare the rest of the numbers.

3. Start from the left. Compare until you find digits that are different.

$$750,50\mathbf{0}$$
$$750,50\mathbf{9}$$

4. Which two digits are different? _____

5. Which of these digits is greater? _____ > _____

6. Which of the numbers is greater? _____ > _____

Step 3 Order the numbers from greatest to least.

7. Write the numbers from greatest to least.

_____

8. Who has the most points? _____

9. Who has the fewest points? _____

Practice

Order the numbers from greatest to least.

1   501,324   1,501,324   1,509,324   51,324

_____

2   26,490   490   6,489   6,490

_____

Fill in the blank with < or >.

3   35,890 ___ 35,790   4   9,408 ___ 9,400   5   1,671,489 ___ 1,671

6   599 ___ 5,999   7   85,310 ___ 185,310   8   790,511 ___ 791,511

9   Jessie's mother traveled 35,002 miles last year on business. Carly's father traveled 35,202 miles. Taylor's uncle traveled 135,002 miles. Who traveled the greatest distance?_____

Who traveled the least distance? _____

10 Order from least to greatest: 3,300,300   303,333   3,303,300

_____   _____   _____

Short Response Question

11 Annie's city has a population of 1,500,000. Laurie's city has a population of 500,000 and Ken's city has a population of 1,499,999. Put the cities in order from greatest to least population. Explain your answer.

_____   _____   _____

_____

_____

Lesson 2.15 ▪ Fractions with denominators 2, 3, 4, 5, 6, 8, 10, 12

 Think About It

When fractions have the same denominator, they can be ordered by looking at the numerators. How can fractions with different denominators be ordered? How would you order the following from greatest to least?

$$\frac{1}{4} \qquad \frac{1}{5} \qquad \frac{8}{10} \qquad \frac{3}{5}$$

 Here's How

Compare fractions with the same denominators.

$\frac{1}{5}$ and _____ have the same denominator. Compare the numerators.

___ < ___ so $\frac{1}{5}$ ___ $\frac{3}{5}$.

Compare fractions with the same numerators.

We know that $\frac{1}{4}$ is greater than $\frac{1}{5}$ by comparing the denominators. The greater the denominator, the smaller the size of each piece.

Compare fractions with different denominators and different numerators.

Is $\frac{1}{4}$ greater than or less than $\frac{3}{5}$? Change the fractions to fractions with the same denominator.

$$\frac{1 \times 5 = 5}{4 \times 5 = 20} \qquad \frac{3 \times 4 = 12}{5 \times 4 = 20} \qquad \frac{5}{20} < \frac{12}{20} \qquad \frac{1}{4} \underline{\quad} \frac{3}{5}$$

Is $\frac{8}{10}$ greater or less than $\frac{3}{5}$?

$$\frac{3 \times 2 = 6}{5 \times 2 = 10} \qquad \frac{8}{10} > \frac{6}{10} \qquad \frac{8}{10} \underline{\quad} \frac{3}{5}$$

Order the fractions from greatest to least. _____

Practice

Order the fractions from greatest to least. Show your work.

1 $\frac{3}{5}, \frac{3}{4}, \frac{1}{2}, \frac{4}{5}, \frac{9}{10}$ _____

2 $\frac{1}{3}, \frac{4}{6}, \frac{5}{12}, \frac{5}{6}$ _____

3 $\frac{1}{2}, \frac{6}{8}, \frac{1}{4}, \frac{3}{8}$ _____

4 The shaded pieces have been eaten. Which pie is closest to $\frac{1}{2}$ eaten?

A 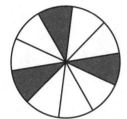 **B**  **C** 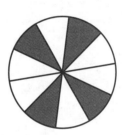 **D**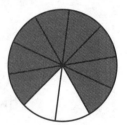

Short Response Question

5 The reading assignment is a book about horses. Brad has read $\frac{3}{5}$ of the book, Lynn has read $\frac{3}{4}$ of the book, and Gwen has read $\frac{3}{10}$ of the book. List the students in order from the fewest pages read to the most pages read. Show your work and explain your answer.

_____

_____

_____

Lesson 2.16 ▪ Decimals to hundredths

Think About It

Emily's apples weigh 2.51 pounds. Jason's apples weigh 2.58 pounds. Whose apples weigh more? Two other friends have apples that weigh 2.55 and 2.57 pounds each. How would you order these numbers from the greatest weight to least weight?

Here's How

Use a place value chart or line up the decimals.

Step 1 Write the numbers in the chart.

Step 2 Begin at the left. Compare the digits in the same place value. Continue comparing to the right until the digits are different. If they are all the same, the numbers are equal.

ones		tenths	hundredths
2	**.**	**5**	**1**
	.		
	.		
	.		

1. What digit is in the ones place in each number? _____

2. What digit is in the tenths place in each number? _____

3. What digit is in the hundredths place in the first number? _____ second number? _____ third number? _____ fourth number? _____

Step 3 Compare the numbers that are different. Use < or >.

4. 1 ____ 8, so 2.51 ____ 2.58. _____'s apples weigh more.

5. 5 ____ 8 and 5 ____ 1. So the order of the three is 2.58, 2.55, 2.51.

6. 7 ____ 8 and 7 ____ 5.

So the order from greatest to least is 2.58, 2.57, 2.55, 2.51.

🔑 Practice

Compare the following numbers and write $<$ or $>$ in the blank.

1 1.88 ___ 1.89   **2** 21.07 ___ 21.70   **3** .55 ___ .57   **4** 89.33 ___ 89.30

5 7.21 ___ 7.12   **6** 15.05 ___ 15.50   **7** 19.86 ___ 19.76   **8** 3.41 ___ 3.14

Compare the following numbers and order them from greatest to least.

9 8.90, 8.09, 8.99, 8.19 _____, _____, _____, _____

10 12.1, 12.01, 12.02, .99 _____, _____, _____, _____

11 3.52, 2.59, 3.51, 3.50 _____, _____, _____, _____

Compare the following numbers and order them from least to greatest.

12 59.65, 59.60, 59.59, 60.60 _____, _____, _____, _____

13 4.89, 4.09, 4.99, 4.90 _____, _____, _____, _____

Short Response Question

14 You are asked to make a sign for a new sandwich shop. It will list several items with their prices.

Ham and Swiss $2.75   Tuna Salad $2.35   Soup of the Day $1.50
Dill Pickle $0.65   Cold Cut $1.65   Oatmeal Cookie $0.50
Potato Salad $0.99   Turkey Breast $2.85   Ice Cream $1.25
Brownie $1.10   Chicken Salad $2.45   Chips $0.55

List all the sandwiches below. Put them in order by price, from greatest to least. Then list the side orders and desserts in the same way.

Sandwiches	Side Orders	Desserts

Lesson 2.17 ▪ Percents that are multiples of 5

> **READY REFERENCE**
> **percent** one part of a hundred; *example,* 80 percent is 80 parts of a hundred
> **%** percent

🗝 Think About It

Carly needs 100 stamps to complete her collection. She has 70 stamps. What percent of the 100 stamps does Carly have so far?

🗝 Here's How

Write as a fraction or a decimal.

1. Carly has 70 stamps out of the 100 she needs. She has $\frac{70}{100}$ or .70.

2. A fraction with a denominator of 100 can be expressed as a percent, so $\frac{70}{100}$ or .70 is the same as 70%.

   Carly has ____% of the stamps she needs.

🗝 Practice

Write each of the fractions as a decimal and as a percent.

1 $\frac{35}{100}$ ·____

____%

2 $\frac{75}{100}$ ·____

____%

3 $\frac{40}{100}$ ·____

____%

4 $\frac{85}{100}$ ·____

____%

5 Jennifer has 100 beads. 25 of the beads are gold, 35 beads are blue, and 40 beads are black.

____ % gold beads ____% blue beads ____% black beads

 6 100 students voted for new school uniforms. 15% voted for black uniforms, 75% voted for blue uniforms, and 10% voted for red uniforms. How many students voted for black uniforms?

A 15 **B** 51 **C** 5 **D** 10

How many students voted for red uniforms?

F 1 **G** 15 **H** 10 **J** 75

7 A survey of 100 fourth-grade students was conducted to determine how many students ride bicycles. 65 of the students have responded. What percent of the group have not responded? Show your work.

_____ % have not responded.

8 $\frac{11}{20}$ of Amy's garden is flowers, $\frac{7}{20}$ of the garden is vegetables, and $\frac{2}{20}$ of the garden is herbs.

____% flowers   ____% vegetables   ____% herbs

9 Jenny has finished 50% of a 300-piece puzzle. How many pieces does she have left? Show your work. _____

10 What percent of the circle is shaded in?

A 2%   **B** 25%   **C** 20%   **D** 50%

Short Response Question

11 A math test has 100 questions. The teacher put the number of correct answers on each paper. He wrote the following information on the board.

Letter grade	% of correct answers
A	95–100%
B	85–94%
C	75–84%
D	65–74%

Your test shows a score of 85. How many questions did you get right? _____
What letter grade would you receive? Explain your answer.

_____

_____

_____

Lesson 2.18 • Ratio in the real world

> **READY REFERENCE**
> **ratio** the comparison of two numbers

 Think About It

What is the ratio of cars to trucks? What is the ratio of trucks to cars?

 Here's How

Step 1 How many cars are there? _____ How many trucks are there? _____

Step 2 Write the ratio of cars to trucks in 3 different ways.

    1. 5 cars to 3 trucks

    2. 5 cars : 3 trucks

    3. $\dfrac{5 \text{ cars}}{3 \text{ trucks}}$

Step 3 Write the ratio of trucks to cars in 3 different ways.

    1. 3 trucks to _____   2. _____ : 5 cars   3. $\dfrac{3}{\rule{1cm}{0.4pt}}$

If a ratio written as a fraction has a denominator of 100, it can be expressed as a percent. *Example:* $\frac{8}{100} = 8\%$; $\frac{100}{100} = 100\%$.

Practice

Write each ratio three ways.

1 56 blue marbles to 72 red marbles   **2** 9 bagels to 15 rolls

_____ _____   _____ _____

_____ _____   _____ _____

3 5 giraffes to 10 bears

_____   _____

_____

4 6 basketballs to 8 baseballs

_____   _____

_____

5 In Jan's school, each classroom has 21 students and 1 teacher. What is the ratio of students to teachers?

A 21 to 2   **B** 21 to 1   **C** 1 to 21   **D** 1 to 1

What is the ratio of teachers to students?

F 1 to 21   **G** 1 : 21   **H** $\frac{1}{21}$ **J** All of the answers

6 Katie is decorating her birthday party with balloons. She has 26 purple balloons and 10 lavender balloons. What is the ratio of purple balloons to lavender balloons?

_____

7 The class took a vote on whether to stay inside or go outside for recess. 15 voted to stay inside and 4 voted to go outside. What was the ratio of votes to go outside to votes to stay in?

_____

Short Response Question

8 Taylor has 3 cousins who live in England. Two cousins are boys and 1 cousin is a girl. He has 7 cousins who live in Kansas. 5 cousins are girls and 2 cousins are boys. What is the ratio of total boy cousins to total girl cousins? Write the ratio in 3 different ways. Then write the ratio of girl cousins to boy cousins.

Boy cousins to girl cousins	Girl cousins to boy cousins

Directions
Use a separate piece of paper to show your work.

1 Denise is entering her dog in a show. There are 41 contestants in front of her in line. What is her position in the line? Write the ordinal number.

Answer _____

2 Fill in the blanks.

$\frac{1}{4}$ dollar = ____ cents or $ ____

$\frac{1}{2}$ dollar = ____ cents or $ ____

3 Which answer has an even number of cookies?

A

B

C

D

4 Adelle ate 2 pieces of pizza and told Kim that she ate $\frac{1}{4}$ of the pizza. Kim disagreed and said she ate $\frac{2}{8}$ of the pizza. Who was right? Explain.

Answer _____

_____

_____

5 What is the value of the digit 7 in the number 1,507,922.14?

F   7,000,000   H   7,000
G   07   J   700

6 Order $\frac{2}{3}$, $\frac{7}{12}$, $\frac{3}{4}$, $\frac{5}{6}$ from least to greatest.

Answer _____

7 Compare 3.01, 1.03, 3.10, and 3.11. Order them from greatest to least.

Answer _____

8 Write the ratio of planes to ships in 3 different ways.

Answer _____

_____

_____

9 One hundred students are attending the county fair. Twenty five students want to ride the roller coaster. What percent of the students want to ride the roller coaster?

Answer _____

Lesson 3.1 • Addition and subtraction of whole numbers

> **READY REFERENCE**
> **addition** finding the sum of two or more numbers
> **subtraction** finding the difference between two numbers
> **regroup** in addition, moving one or more tens from the ones column, or moving one or more hundreds from the tens column, and so on; in subtraction, moving one ten to the ones column, one hundred to the tens column, and so on
> **rounding** writing a number as the nearest ten or hundred, and so on

 Think About It

This morning you counted 539 sports cards in your collection. A surprise package just arrived with 375 more cards. How many do you have now? Help a friend start a collection by giving him 185 of your cards. How many cards do you have left?

 Here's How

Add 539 plus 375. Estimate first by rounding. _____ + _____ = _____

Step 1 Add the ones. Regroup 14 ones as 1 ten 4 ones.

$$
\begin{array}{r}
1 \\
539 \\
+\,375 \\
\hline
\end{array}
$$

Step 2 Add the tens. Regroup 11 tens as 1 hundred 1 ten.

$$
\begin{array}{r}
1\,1 \\
539 \\
+\,375 \\
\hline
4
\end{array}
$$

Step 3 Add the hundreds.

$$
\begin{array}{r}
1\,1 \\
539 \\
+\,375 \\
\hline
14
\end{array}
$$

Step 4 Compare the answer and your estimate.

Subtract 185 from 914. Estimate first by rounding. _____ − _____ = _____

Step 5 Subtract the ones. Regroup 1 ten as 10 ones.

$$
\begin{array}{r}
0\ 14 \\
9\cancel{1}\cancel{4} \\
-\,185 \\
\hline
\end{array}
$$

Step 6 Subtract the tens. Regroup 1 hundred as 10 tens.

$$
\begin{array}{r}
8\ 10\ 14 \\
9\cancel{1}\cancel{4} \\
-\,185 \\
\hline
9
\end{array}
$$

Step 7 Subtract the hundreds.

```
  8 1014
  9̸X̸A̸
− 185
 729
```

Step 8 Compare the answer and your estimate. Are they close? Check by adding the difference and the number you subtracted. The sum should equal the number you subtracted from.

What numbers did you add to check your answer? _____ + _____

Practice

Solve the problems.

1
```
  88
+ 49
```

2
```
  417
+ 268
```

3
```
  6,789
+ 1,122
```

4
```
  49,168
+ 36,216
```

5
```
  312,334
+ 123,437
```

6
```
  72
− 38
```

7
```
  988
− 769
```

8
```
  7,126
− 3,652
```

9
```
  28,156
− 13,197
```

10
```
  459,611
− 254,326
```

Write the problem in numbers and find the answer. Check your answer.

11 Roddy has 356 soccer cards and 289 football cards. How many sports cards does he have in all?

_____

12 Annie has 2,695 pennies in a jar. She wants to surprise her little sister by giving her 958 pennies. How many will Annie have left?

_____

Short Response Question

13 Carlos collects toy cars and toy trucks. He has 58 toy cars and 37 toy trucks. Carlos decides to give a friend 16 of his cars and trucks. How many toy cars and trucks does Carlos have before he gave any away? _____ How many will he have left? _____ Show your work.

Lesson 3.2 ▪ Subtracting with zeroes in the minuend

Think About It

Maria's favorite video game requires 3,000 points to move from the first level to the second level. She scored 1,836 points. How many more points does she need to score to move to the second level?

Here's How

Subtract 1,836 from 3,000. Estimate first by rounding. _____ − _____ = _____

Step 1 There are no ones, tens, or hundreds to subtract. Regroup 1 thousand as 10 hundreds.

$$\begin{array}{r} \overset{2\ \ 10}{\cancel{3},000} \\ -\ 1,836 \end{array}$$

Step 2 Regroup 1 hundred as 10 tens.

$$\begin{array}{r} \overset{9}{\overset{2\ \cancel{10}\,10}{\cancel{3},000}} \\ -\ 1,836 \end{array}$$

Step 3 Regroup 1 ten as 10 ones.

$$\begin{array}{r} \overset{9\ 9}{\overset{2\ \cancel{10}\cancel{10}\,10}{\cancel{3},000}} \\ -\ 1,836 \end{array}$$

Step 4 Subtract. Write the answer.

$$\begin{array}{r} \overset{9\ 9}{\overset{2\ \cancel{10}\cancel{10}\,10}{\cancel{3},000}} \\ -\ 1,836 \end{array}$$

Step 5 Compare the answer and your estimate.

Check by adding.

$$\begin{array}{r} 1,164 \\ +\ 1,836 \end{array}$$

Does the sum equal the number you subtracted from?

_____

Practice

Solve the problems.

1
$$\begin{array}{r} 400 \\ -\ 127 \end{array}$$

2
$$\begin{array}{r} 502 \\ -\ 235 \end{array}$$

3
$$\begin{array}{r} 700 \\ -\ 308 \end{array}$$

4
$$\begin{array}{r} 520 \\ -\ 75 \end{array}$$

5
$$\begin{array}{r} 600 \\ -\ 230 \end{array}$$

6 900
  − 368

7 3,000
  − 1,256

8 9,000
  − 274

9 4,000
  − 2,673

10 60,906
  − 46,346

11 8,060
  − 3,360

12 4,000
  − 2,160

13 6,500
  − 541

14 7,000
  − 3,218

15 3,000
  − 1,057

16 40,030
  − 17,568

17 87,000
  − 68,781

18 50,002
  − 20,658

19 90,094
  − 6,863

20 80,800
  − 21,670

Write the problem in numbers and find the answer.

21 Joe is reading an exciting adventure book that has 200 pages. He has read 89 pages. How many pages does he have left to finish the book?

_____

22 Anita scored 8,000 points in a math tournament. Her best friend scored 6,352 points. How many more points did Anita score than her friend?

_____

Short Response Question

23 Your family is working on a 5,000-piece puzzle of the United States. You have 3,859 pieces left to use. How many pieces have already been used? Show your work and explain your steps.

_____

_____

_____

Lesson 3.3 ▪ Multiply three-digit numbers by two-digit numbers

> **READY REFERENCE**
>
> **multiplication** an operation that uses two or more numbers, called factors, to find the answer, called the product
>
> **factor** the numbers that are multiplied to find a product
>
> **product** the answer in multiplication
>
> **regroup** use 1 ten to form 10 ones, 1 hundred to form 10 tens, and so on

Think About It

Do you ride the bus to school? If you ride the bus to school 181 days in a year and spend 32 minutes per day on the bus, how many minutes do you spend on the school bus each year?

Here's How

Step 1 Multiply by the ones. Regroup if necessary.

$\begin{array}{r} 181 \\ \times\ 32 \\ \hline \end{array}$

    1. What is the product of multiplying by the ones? _____

    2. Did you have to regroup? _____

Step 2 Place a 0 in the ones place. Multiply by the tens. Regroup if you can.

$\begin{array}{r} ^1\ \ \\ 181 \\ \times\ 32 \\ \hline 362 \\ 0 \\ \hline \end{array}$

    3. Did you need to regroup? _____

Step 3 Add the products.

    4. What is the product? _____

Practice

1 $\begin{array}{r} 757 \\ \times\ 34 \\ \hline \end{array}$

2 $\begin{array}{r} 329 \\ \times\ 17 \\ \hline \end{array}$

3 $\begin{array}{r} 23 \\ \times\ 40 \\ \hline \end{array}$

4 $\begin{array}{r} 174 \\ \times\ 55 \\ \hline \end{array}$

5 $\begin{array}{r} 666 \\ \times\ 60 \\ \hline \end{array}$

6 822
× 13

7 645
× 27

8 299
× 42

9 381
× 68

10 277
× 50

11 498
× 11

12 705
× 47

13 393
× 82

14 480
× 35

15 129
× 46

Write the problem in numbers and find the answer.

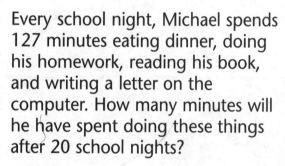

16 Every school night, Michael spends 127 minutes eating dinner, doing his homework, reading his book, and writing a letter on the computer. How many minutes will he have spent doing these things after 20 school nights?

<u>2540 minutes</u>

17 Every day, the people in the Sit Down Chair Factory make 88 chairs. How many chairs do they make in 2 years if they work 352 days each year?

_____

Short Response Question

18 Every day, Charlotte, Kate, and Amanda practice playing their flutes. The table below shows how much time each girl spends playing every day. Complete the table to show how many minutes each girl practices. Explain how you completed the table.

Student	Min. per day	Min. in 7 days	Min. in 30 days	Min. in a year (365 days)
Charlotte	33	231	990	12045
Kate	38			
Amanda	40			

_____

_____

_____

Lesson 3.4 ▪ Division of three-digit dividends

> **READY REFERENCE**
> **dividend** the number to be divided
> **divisor** the number by which another number is divided
> **quotient** the answer in division

 Think About It

The fourth-grade class is planning a talent show for the entire school. The talent presentations will last a total of 190 minutes. Twenty-one students signed up to be in the talent show. How much time will each student have to perform?

 Here's How

Divide 190 by 21.

Step 1 There are not enough hundreds to divide into 21 groups. There are not enough tens to divide into 21 groups. Regroup 1 hundred 9 tens 0 ones as 190 ones.

$$21\overline{)190}$$

Step 2 Divide the ones. Multiply and subtract. Compare the difference (remainder) to the divisor. The difference must be less than the divisor. Write the remainder next to the quotient.

$$\begin{array}{r} 9 \text{ R1} \\ 21\overline{)190} \\ -189 \quad 9 \times 21 \\ \hline \text{remainder } (1{<}21) \end{array}$$

Step 3 Check by multiplying the divisor by the quotient. Add the remainder to that product.

$$
\begin{array}{rl}
21 & \leftarrow \text{ divisor} \\
\times 9 & \leftarrow \text{ quotient} \\
\hline
189 & \leftarrow \text{ product} \\
+1 & \leftarrow \text{ remainder} \\
\hline
190 & \leftarrow \text{ should be the same as} \\
& \text{ the dividend}
\end{array}
$$

🔑 Practice

1 $4\overline{)382}$ **2** $7\overline{)463}$ **3** $5\overline{)309}$ **4** $8\overline{)690}$ **5** $2\overline{)225}$

6 $82\overline{)663}$ **7** $61\overline{)491}$ **8** $21\overline{)178}$ **9** $72\overline{)580}$ **10** $39\overline{)138}$

Write the problem in numbers and find the answer.

11 There are 592 people who want to see a play. The theater has 26 rows. How many people can sit in each row?

_____

How many people will not be able to see the play?

_____

12 The fourth-grade production of "89 Cats" has been so successful that 325 tickets have been sold. The auditorium can seat 65 people. How many performances must be held?

_____

Short Response Question

13 The Break a Leg drama class decided that each member has to sell the same number of tickets. There are 323 tickets and 21 members. How many tickets must each member sell? Will there be any left over? Explain your answer and show your work.

_____

_____

_____

_____

Lesson 3.5 ▪ Using diagrams and tables

🔑 Think About It

Diagrams and tables can help us solve problems. They help us organize and understand information. Facts can be shown in tables such as the one below. Red was the favorite color of 5 boys and 4 girls. Blue was the favorite of 3 girls and 4 boys. Green was the favorite of 2 boys and 2 girls.

Favorite Colors			
	Boys	Girls	Total
Red	5	4	9
Blue			
Green			

🔑 Here's How

Use a table.

Step 1 Look at the problem and the table.

1. How many colors were studied in the survey? _____

2. What does the table show? _____

Step 2 Divide the facts into groups.

3. How many boys chose red? _____

4. How many girls chose red? _____

5. How many total students chose red? _____

Step 3 Put the facts into a table.

6. Reread the sentences about the favorite colors. Complete the table by adding the information for blue and green under the correct headings.

7. What is the favorite color of this class? _____

Use a tree diagram.

For lunch there are two main dishes and three side dishes. Each student must choose a main dish and a side dish. How many kinds of meals can the students choose from?

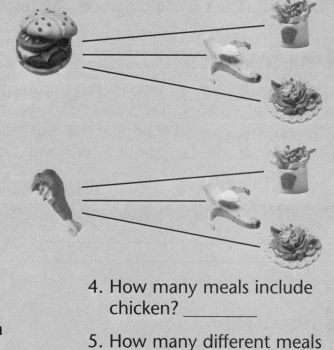

Step 1   Study the tree diagram.

   1. How many main dishes are there? _____

   2. How many side dishes are there? _____

Step 2   Divide the facts into groups.

   3. How many meals include a hamburger? _____

   4. How many meals include chicken? _____

   5. How many different meals can students choose from?

   _____

Practice

1 Charles can choose a rose, a tulip, a carnation, or a daisy. He can choose a pink, yellow, orange, or purple pot for the plant. How many different choices of plants and pots does he have? (Hint: draw a tree diagram to solve this problem.)

_____

2 Look through a book about animals. How many different kinds of animals are shown? How are these animals alike and different? List three groups of animals. Which group has the most animals in it? (Hint: make a table to sort the information.)

_____

Short Response Question

3 Find out how your classmates get to school. Find the method of transportation used by the most students and the method used by the least. Explain how you would solve this problem.

_____

_____

Lesson 3.6 ▪ Open sentences

> **READY REFERENCE**
> **open sentence** a problem in which a number is missing and must be identified
> **variable** a letter used to represent a missing number in an open sentence

 Think About It

The *x* and *y* represent a number that you don't know. This is the number you have to find. What numbers should replace the *x* and *y* in these open sentences? Letters called variables can be used to represent a missing number in a sentence. Any letter of the alphabet can be used as a variable.

$$5 + x = 12$$
$$7 \times y = 35$$

 Here's How

Lin Wong has 6 videos to return to the video store. Her father asked her to return some of his videos. Lin returned 10 videos to the store. How many videos did Lin's father ask her to return?

Solve using addition.

Step 1 Write an open number sentence to solve the problem. Make *x* stand for the number of Lin's father's videos.

$$\_\_\_ + x = 10$$

Step 2 Solve the problem.

$$6 + x = 10$$

What number equals *x*?

$$x = \_\_\_$$

Solve using subtraction.

Step 1 Write an open number sentence.

$$10 - \_\_\_ = x$$

Step 2 What number equals *x*?

$$x = \_\_\_$$

Larry's mother asked him to plant 28 tulip bulbs. He planted 7 bulbs in each row. How many rows did he plant? Let m represent the number of rows.

Solve using multiplication.

Step 1 Write an open number sentence.

You could write a multiplication sentence to solve this problem.

$7 \times m = 28$ or $7m = 28$

Step 2 Solve the problem.

$m = $ _____

Solve using division.

Step 1 Write an open number sentence.

$28 \div m = 7$ or $28 \div 7 = m$

Step 2 Solve the problem.

$m = $ _____

🔑 Practice

Write an open sentence for each problem. Solve the problem.

1 Five times a number is 20. What is the number?

_____

2 Kerry runs a children's summer camp. There are 8 camp sessions scheduled. The same number of campers will attend each session. There are 160 total campers. How many will attend each session?

_____

Short Response Question

3 Read each problem and follow the directions.

Part A Write a word problem for the open number sentence $36 \div x = 9$

_____

_____

Part B Solve the word problem you wrote for the number sentence and explain your work.

_____

_____

Lesson 3.7 ▪ Commutative, associative, distributive, and inverse properties

> **READY REFERENCE**
>
> **commutative property** two or more numbers can be added in any order and two numbers can be multiplied in any order
>
> **associative property** more than two numbers can be added in groups of two in any order and more than two numbers can be multiplied in groups of two in any order
>
> **distributive property** to multiply a sum or difference by a number, multiply each number of the sum or difference separately
>
> **inverse operations** two operations with the opposite effect; addition is the inverse operation of subtraction; multiplication is the inverse operation of division

 Think About It

Knowing different properties of addition, subtraction, multiplication, and division will help you choose the best method to solve math problems quickly.

 Here's How

Commutative Property of Addition

$85 + 33 = 118$ or $33 + \_\_\_\_ = 118$

So $85 + 33 = 33 + \_\_\_\_$

Commutative Property of Multiplication

$7 \times 3 = 21$ or $\_\_\_\_ \times 7 = 21$

So $7 \times 3 = \_\_\_\_ \times 7$

Associative Property of Addition

$(1 + 2) + 7 = 10$ or $\_\_\_\_ + (2 + 7) = 10$

So $(1 + 2) + 7 = \_\_\_\_ + (2 + 7)$

Associative Property of Multiplication

$2 \times (3 \times 4) = 24$ or $(2 \times 3) \times \_\_\_\_ = 24$

So $2 \times (3 \times 4) = (2 \times 3) \times \_\_\_\_$

Distributive Property

$2(4 + 5) = 18$ *or* $(2 \times 4) + (\underline{\quad} \times 5) = 18$

  So $2(4 + 5) = (2 \times 4) + (\underline{\quad} \times 5)$

$3(20 - 2) = 54$ *or* $(\underline{\quad} \times 20) - (3 \times 2) = 54$

  So $3(20 - 2) = (\underline{\quad} \times 20) - (3 \times 2)$

Inverse Property

$(6 + 2) - 2 = 6$ *or* $(\underline{\quad} - 2) + 2 = 6$

  So $(6 + 2) - 2 = (\underline{\quad} - 2) + 2$

$(20 \times 5) \div 5 = 20$ *or* $(20 \div 5) \times \underline{\quad} = 20$

  So $(20 \times 5) \div 5 = (20 \div 5) \times \underline{\quad}$

🔑 Practice

Write the name of the property on the line.

1 $6 \times 4 = 4 \times 6$

_____

2 $8 + (2 + 5) = (8 + 2) + 5$

_____

3 $(4 - 2) + 2 = (4 + 2) - 2$

_____

4 $3(4 + 2) = (3 \times 4) + (3 \times 2)$

_____

Complete the following open number sentences.

5 $(4 \times \underline{\quad}) \div 2 = 4$

6 $2(3 + 2) = 2 \times 3 + \underline{\quad} \times 2$

7 $4(2 - 1) = 4 \times 2 \underline{\quad} 4 \times 1$

8 $(6 \div 2) \times \underline{\quad} = 6$

9 $(12 \times 2) \div 2 = \underline{\quad}$

10 $(4 \times 5) \times 2 = 4 \times (\underline{\quad} \times 2) = \underline{\quad}$

Short Response Question

11 If the order of the addends in an addition problem changes, does the sum change? Write a problem to illustrate your answer.

_____

_____

Lesson 3.8 ▪ Look for patterns

READY REFERENCE
pattern a series of items or actions that appear or happen in a specific order
relationship the characteristic that items in a pattern share with each other
sequence the order in which the items in a pattern are arranged

Think About It

Patterns are everywhere in the world. Special relationships between items make patterns. How often these relationships happen affect the pattern's order, or sequence.

Here's How

Pattern A 2, 4, 6, 8, 10, . . .   **Pattern B** 15, 12, 9, 6, . . .
Pattern C 1, 2, 4, 8, 16, 32, . . .

Step 1 First, examine the relationships in each pattern.

1. Which patterns are made up of a series of numbers?_____

Step 2 Next, identify the sequence of the relationships.

2. Which numerical patterns have numbers that increase in value?_____
Which one decreases in value?_____

3. How much does each number increase or decrease in value in each numerical pattern?

A _____   B _____   C _____

Step 3 Use sequence to predict, or extend, the pattern.

4. What will be the next number in each numerical pattern?

A _____   B _____   C _____

Practice

1. Write the missing numbers in the following patterns.

   45, 43, 41, _____ , 37, 35, 33, _____

   16, 20, 24, 28, _____ , 36, _____

2. Describe the pattern in the quotient when 9, 90, 900, and 9,000 are each divided by 3.

   _____

3. Describe the pattern in the product when the following are multiplied.

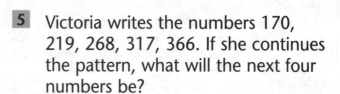

   $4 \times 3 =$ _12_ $4 \times 30 =$ _100_ $4 \times 300 =$ _1200_ $4 \times 3,000 =$ _12000_

   _____

4. How many rows can you make if you continue the pattern below to 36 triangles?

   _____

5. Victoria writes the numbers 170, 219, 268, 317, 366. If she continues the pattern, what will the next four numbers be?

   _____

Short Response Question

6. Make up your own numerical pattern and write it on the first line below. What is the relationship among the items of your numerical pattern? How will the sequence of the items show in this relationship? Write a description explaining your pattern.

   _____

   _____

   _____

Lesson 3.9 ▪ Breaking a problem into parts

Think About It

Did you ever give someone step-by-step instructions about how to do something? Many math problems can be broken into parts, or steps, which makes the problem easier to solve.

Here's How

Mr. Parker had to replace a total of 11 window shades in 3 rooms. In one room, he replaced 3 window shades. In the second room, he replaced twice as many. How many did he replace in the third room?

Step 1 List the things you know.

1. A total of _____ window shades were replaced in 3 rooms.

2. In the first room, _____ were replaced.

3. In the second room, _____ × 3 were replaced.

Step 2 Write what you need to find out.

4. _____

Step 3 Make a plan using steps.

5. Find the number of window shades replaced in the second room.

_____ × 3 = _____

6. Add the number replaced in the first and second rooms.

_____ + 6 = _____

7. Subtract the number replaced in the first two rooms from the total number of window shades that were replaced.

11 − _____ = x

Step 4 Solve the problem.

8. How many window shades were replaced in the third room? _____

🔑 Practice

1 Cesar's spelling book has 156 pages. Half of his math book is 15 pages longer than his spelling book. How many pages does Cesar's math book contain?

_____

2 The six grades at Big Valley Elementary School sold 200 tickets to pay for their school carnival. Grades 1, 2, and 3 each sold 22 tickets. Grade 4 sold 52 tickets. Grade 5 sold 10 tickets less than Grade 4. How many tickets did Grade 6 sell?

_____

Extended Response Question
Read the problem. Break the problem into parts to solve it. Show your work.

3 Yesterday morning, Crissie counted 14 sailboats and 18 ski boats that sailed into the cove. Yesterday afternoon, she counted three times as many sailboats, but only half as many ski boats. How many sailboats and ski boats did Crissie count all together?

List the things you know. _____

_____

_____

Write what you need to find out.

_____

_____

Make a plan using steps. (Add steps on your own paper if necessary.)

1. _____

2. _____

3. _____

Lesson 3.10 ▪ Inverse relationships of operations

> **READY REFERENCE**
>
> **inverse operations** two operations with the opposite effect; addition is the inverse operation of subtraction; multiplication is the inverse operation of division

⚷ Think About It

Addition and subtraction are inverse operations. Addition has the opposite effect of subtraction. Subtraction has the opposite effect of addition. They "undo" each other. Multiplication and division are inverse operations. Multiplication has the opposite effect of division. Division has the opposite effect of multiplication. They "undo" each other. This is why we can use addition to check subtraction, subtraction to check addition, multiplication to check division, and division to check multiplication.

⚷ Here's How

Addition and subtraction are inverse operations.		
When you check addition with two addends, subtract one addend from the sum. The answer is the other addend.	$\begin{array}{r} 347 \\ +\ 201 \\ \hline 548 \end{array}$	$\begin{array}{r} 548 \\ -\ 201 \\ \hline 347 \end{array}$
When you check subtraction, add the difference and the minuend. The answer is the subtrahend.	$\begin{array}{r} 968 \\ -\ 414 \\ \hline 554 \end{array}$	$\begin{array}{r} 554 \\ +\ 414 \\ \hline 968 \end{array}$
Multiplication and division are inverse operations.		
When you check multiplication, divide the product by one of the factors. The answer is the other factor.	$\begin{array}{r} 212 \\ \times\ 12 \\ \hline 2{,}544 \end{array}$	$2{,}544 \div 12 = 212$
When you check division, multiply the quotient by the divisor. The answer is the dividend.	$2{,}905 \div 7 = 415$ $415 \times 7 = 2{,}905$	

🔑 Practice

1 What is the inverse operation of addition?

_____

2 What is the inverse operation of multiplication?

_____

Write the inverse operation for the following problems.

3 $3 + 5 = 8$ _____

4 $2 \times 4 = 8$ _____

5 $9 - 4 = 5$ _____

6 $6 \div 3 = 2$ _____

7 $2 + 5 = 7$ _____

8 $3 \times 3 = 9$ _____

9 Which of the following is the inverse operation for $4 + 3 = 7$?

A $7 + 3 = 10$

B $7 - 3 = 4$

C $3 + 4 = 7$

D $4 \times 3 = 12$

10 Which of the following is the inverse operation for $3 \times 2 = 6$?

F $6 \div 2 = 3$

G $6 \times 2 = 12$

H $2 \times 3 = 6$

J $3 + 2 = 5$

11 Which of the following is the inverse operation for $7 - 5 = 2$?

A $7 - 2 = 5$

B $2 + 5 = 7$

C $7 \times 2 = 14$

D $2 + 7 = 9$

12 Which of the following is the inverse operation for $9 \div 3 = 3$?

F $9 \times 3 = 27$

G $3 + 3 = 6$

H $6 + 3 = 9$

J $3 \times 3 = 9$

Short Response Question

13 Write three addition problems and three subtraction problems. Solve the problems. Write the inverse operation for each problem.

Lesson 3.11 ▪ Special role of zero

 Think About It

Knowing facts and rules about zero is important when solving even simple problems.

 Here's How

Addition and zero
The sum of 0 and a number is the same as the number. $5 + 0 = 5$

Subtraction and zero
When 0 is subtracted from a number, the difference $5 - 0 = 5$
  is that same number.

Multiplication and zero
When 0 is multiplied by any number, the $5 \times 0 = 0 \quad 0 \times 5 = 0$
  product is 0.

Division and zero
When 0 is divided by any number except 0, $0 \div 5 = 0 \quad 5\overline{)0}$
  the quotient is 0.
You cannot divide a number by 0.

Practice

Answer the questions and write a number sentence for each answer.

1 What is the sum when 0 is added to a number?   _____

2 What is the difference when 0 is subtracted from a number?   _____

3 What is the product when a number is multiplied by 0?   _____

4 What is the product when 0 is multiplied by another number?   _____

5 What is the quotient when 0 is divided by another number?   _____

6 What is the quotient when a number is divided by 0?   _____

Solve the following problems.

7 53
+ 0

8 95
− 0

9 44
× 0

10 18
− 0

11 309
+ 0

12 27
× 0

13 92
× 0

14 983
× 0

15 0 ÷ 268 = _____

16 0 ÷ 15 = _____

17 0 ÷ 88 = _____

18 0 ÷ 74 = _____

19 Nine students and 3 teachers played basketball on Saturday. Each student brought a basketball. None of the teachers brought one. How many basketballs did the group have? Write the problem and solve it.

20 Katrina had 7 popsicles in her freezer. She had 3 friends over to spend the night. Katrina and each of her friends ate 0 popsicles. How many popsicles were left? Write the problem and solve it.

Short Response Question

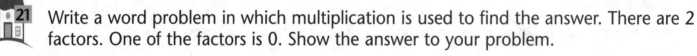

21 Write a word problem in which multiplication is used to find the answer. There are 2 factors. One of the factors is 0. Show the answer to your problem.

_____

_____

_____

Lesson 3.12 ▪ Multiplication and division facts

> **READY REFERENCE**
>
> **identity property** the product of any number and 1 is that number
> $(6 \times 1 = 6)$; any number divided by 1 is that number $(6 \div 1 = 6)$
>
> **fact family** related facts using the same numbers
>
> **pattern** a series of items or actions that appear or happen in a specific order

 Think About It

We use multiplication and division facts often. There are many ways to learn and remember multiplication and division facts.

 Here's How

Multiplication	Division
Use doubles for 4s and 6s. $2 \times 3 = \mathbf{6}$ $\qquad$ $3 \times 4 = \mathbf{12}$ $4 \times 3 = \mathbf{6 + 6}$ $\qquad$ $6 \times 4 = \mathbf{12 + 12}$ $4 \times 3 = \underline{\quad}$ $\qquad$ $6 \times 4 = \underline{\quad}$ **Use addition.** $6 \times 4 = \underline{\quad}$ $4 + 4 + 4 + 4 + 4 + 4 = \underline{\quad}$ **Use skip counting.** $7 \times 5 = \underline{\quad}$ Count by 5s seven times: 5, 10, 15, 20, 25, 30, 35	**Use fact families.** This is the fact family for 4, 6, and 24. $4 \times 6 = \underline{\quad}$ $\qquad$ $\underline{\quad} \times 4 = 24$ $24 \div 4 = \underline{\quad}$ $\qquad$ $24 \div \underline{\quad} = 4$ **Use the identity property.** $5 \div 1 = 5$ $\qquad$ $4 \div \underline{\quad} = 4$ $8 \div 1 = \underline{\quad}$ **Use the zero property.** $0 \div 5 = 0$ $\qquad$ $0 \div 4 = \underline{\quad}$ $0 \div 8 = \underline{\quad}$

Use multiplication patterns (especially for 7s and 9s).

$7 \times 1 = 7$ $7 \times 2 = 14$ $7 \times 3 = 21$

$7 +$ _____ $14 +$ _____

For 9s, the sum of the digits of each product is 9.

$9 \times 3 =$ **27**   **2 + 7** $= 9$

$9 \times 4 =$ **36**   **3 + 6** $=$ _____

🔑 Practice

1 $2 \times 3 =$ _____   **2** $3 \times 4 =$ _____   **3** $3 \times 5 =$ _____   **4** $2 \times 7 =$ _____

     $4 \times 3 =$ _____ $6 \times 4 =$ _____ $6 \times 5 =$ _____ $4 \times 7 =$ _____

5 $0 \times 341 =$ _____   **6** $1 \times 932 =$ _____   **7** $(7 \times 0) \times 6 =$ _____

8 $0 \div 8 =$ _____   **9** $7 \div$ _____ $= 7$ **10** $2 \div 2 =$ _____

11 $\begin{array}{r} 10 \\ \times\, 10 \\ \hline \end{array}$ **12** $\begin{array}{r} 11 \\ \times\, 10 \\ \hline \end{array}$ **13** $\begin{array}{r} 12 \\ \times\, 4 \\ \hline \end{array}$ **14** $\begin{array}{r} 32 \\ \times\, 7 \\ \hline \end{array}$ **15** $\begin{array}{r} 11 \\ \times\, 9 \\ \hline \end{array}$ **16** $\begin{array}{r} 12 \\ \times\, 12 \\ \hline \end{array}$

17 $72 \div 9 =$ _____   **18** $11\overline{)121}$ **19** $85 \div 5 =$ _____   **20** $9\overline{)81}$

Write the fact family for the set of numbers.

21   6, 8, 48   _____   _____   _____   _____

Short Response Question

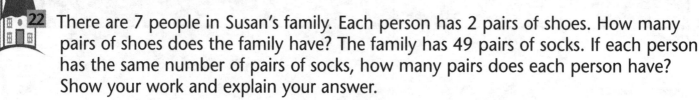

22   There are 7 people in Susan's family. Each person has 2 pairs of shoes. How many pairs of shoes does the family have? The family has 49 pairs of socks. If each person has the same number of pairs of socks, how many pairs does each person have? Show your work and explain your answer.

_____

_____

Lesson 3.13 • Identity elements of addition and multiplication

> **READY REFERENCE**
> **identity element** 0 is the addition identity element, $3 + 0 = 0$; 1 is the multiplication identity element, $3 \times 1 = 3$.

Think About It

Counters can be used throughout this lesson.

If you add 0 to a number, does the number change? What happens when you multiply a number by 1?

Here's How

Addition	Multiplication
Place 6 counters on your desk. Place 0 counters next to the 6. How many counters are on your desk? $6 + 0 = \underline{\hspace{2em}}$	Amy's sister has a new part-time job at the mall. She will make $75 a week. Her first paycheck will be for 1 week's work. How much will her check be? $\$75 \times 1 = \$ \underline{\hspace{2em}}$

Practice

1 $1 \times 89 = \underline{\hspace{2em}}$ **2** $\underline{\hspace{2em}} \times 1 = 40$ **3** $35 + 0 = \underline{\hspace{2em}}$ **4** $23 \times \underline{\hspace{2em}} = 23$

5 $49 + 0 = \underline{\hspace{2em}}$ **6** $\underline{\hspace{2em}} \times 76 = 76$ **7** $56 + \underline{\hspace{2em}} = 56$ **8** $68 \times 1 = \underline{\hspace{2em}}$

Choose the letter for each correct answer.

9 $4 + 0 = \underline{\hspace{2em}}$ **10** $4 \times 1 = \underline{\hspace{2em}}$ **11** $7 + 0 = \underline{\hspace{2em}}$ **12** $3 \times 1 = \underline{\hspace{2em}}$

A 4	**F** 1	**A** 70	**F** 3
B 0	**G** 4	**B** 7	**G** 31
C 1	**H** 0	**C** 0	**H** 1
D 40	**J** none of the above	**D** 71	**J** 0

13 $117 + 0 + 389 + 1 =$ _____

14 $28 \times 4 \times 0 =$ _____

15 Carlos checks his family's mail every day after school. On Monday he picked up 5 letters from the mailbox. On Tuesday he found no letters. How many letters did he pick up in all from the mailbox? Show your work.

_____

16 Christopher loves to attend the state fair. The rides are his favorite part of the fair. There are 9 rides at the fair. This year he was able to attend the fair for only 1 day and ride 1 time on each ride. How many rides did he go on? Show your work.

_____

Short Response Question

17 A set of colored art pencils contains 8 pencils. The set sells for $7. Extra pencils cost $2 each. If Kim Yung buys one set without any extra pencils, how many pencils does she have and how much did she spend? Show and explain your work.

_____

_____

_____

Lesson 3.14 ▪ Commutative property of addition and multiplication

> **READY REFERENCE**
>
> **commutative property of addition** two or more numbers can be added in any order
>
> **commutative property of multiplication** two or more numbers can be multiplied in any order

⚷ Think About It

Ann's aunt gave her 6 apples on Monday. Her uncle gave her 4 apples on Tuesday. How many apples does Ann have? How many apples would Ann have if her aunt gave her 4 apples on Monday and her uncle gave her 6 apples on Tuesday? Does the order of the addends change the sum?

Derek's family is moving to a new neighborhood in 2 weeks. How many days are there until they move? Does it matter whether you multiply *weeks x days* or *days x weeks*? Does the order of the factors change the product?

⚷ Here's How

Commutative Property of Addition	Commutative Property of Multiplication
Place 6 counters on your desk. Place 4 counters next to the 6. How many counters are on your desk? Pick up the counters. Now, place 4 counters on your desk. Place 6 counters next to the 4 counters. How many counters are on your desk?	Use your counters. Make 2 groups with 7 counters in each group. How many counters do you have? Now, make 7 groups with 2 in each group. How many counters do you have?

$6 + 4 = $ _____ $4 + 6 = $ _____

$$\begin{array}{r} 6 \\ +\,4 \\ \hline \end{array} \qquad \begin{array}{r} 4 \\ +\,6 \\ \hline \end{array}$$

If the order of the addends changes, does the sum remain the same?

_____

$2 \times 7 = $ _____ $7 \times 2 = $ _____

$$\begin{array}{r} 2 \\ \times\,7 \\ \hline \end{array} \qquad \begin{array}{r} 7 \\ \times\,2 \\ \hline \end{array}$$

If the order of the factors changes, does the product remain the same?

_____

🔑 Practice

1 $1 \times 3 =$ _____ $\times 1$ **2** $4 + 1 =$ _____ $+ 4$ **3** $3 \times 4 = 4 \times$ _____

4 $2 + 5 =$ _____ $+ 2$ **5** $6 \times 4 =$ _____ $\times 6$ **6** $5 \times 9 = 9 \times$ _____

7 $6 + 8 =$ _____ $+ 6$ **8** $11 \times 5 =$ _____ $\times 11$

9 $4 + 3 =$ _____   **10** $5 \times 4 =$ _____   **11** $7 + 5 =$ _____   **12** $9 \times 6 =$ _____

A $3 + 4$ **F** $5 + 4$ **A** $5 + 7$ **F** 9×3

B 4×3 **G** 4×5 **B** $7 - 5$ **G** 3×8

C $4 \div 3$ **H** 54 **C** 5×7 **H** 6×9

D 34 **J** none of the above   **D** 71 **J** 0

Short Response Question

13 Two fourth-grade classes are taking a field trip to a space museum. The visit includes viewing a movie. The theater seats 35 students. One class has 18 students and the other class has 17 students. Can the theater hold both classes at the same time? Will the order in which the classes are seated make a difference? Show your work and explain your answer.

_____

_____

_____

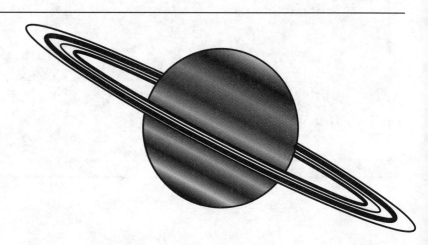

Lesson 3.15 ▪ Associative property of addition and multiplication

> **READY REFERENCE**
>
> **associative property of addition** more than two numbers can be added in groups of two in any order
>
> **associative property of multiplication** more than two numbers can be multiplied in groups of two in any order

🗝 Think About It

◆ Ann's aunt gave her 6 apples. Her uncle gave her 4 apples. Her cousin gave her 2 apples. Add 6 apples and 4 apples. Now add 2 apples. How many apples does Ann have? Add 6 apples and 2 apples. Now add 4 apples. How many apples does Ann have? Add 4 apples and 2 apples. Now add 6 apples. How many apples does Ann have? Did changing the way you group the addends change the sum?

🗝 Here's How

Associative Property of Addition	Associative Property of Multiplication
Place 6 counters on your desk. Place 4 counters next to the 6. How many counters are on your desk? Place 2 more counters on your desk. How many counters are there now? $(6 + 4) + 2 = \underline{\quad}$ $6 + (4 + 2) = \underline{\quad}$ If the grouping of the addends changes, does the sum remain the same? _____	$(2 \times 7) \times 3 = \underline{\quad}$ $2 \times (7 \times 3) = \underline{\quad}$ If the grouping of the factors changes, does the product remain the same? _____

🗝 Practice

1 $(2 \times 3) \times 4 = 2 \,(\underline{\quad} \times 4)$

2 $(4 + 5) + 3 = \underline{\quad} + (5 + 3)$

3 $(12 \times 4) \times 2 = 12 \times (4 \times \underline{\quad})$

4 $6 + (4 + 3) = (\underline{\quad} + 4) + 3$

5 $5 \times (8 \times 4) = ($ _____ $\times 8) \times 4$

6 $(6 + 8) + 11 = 6 + ($ _____ $+ 11)$

Which answer shows the associative property?

7 $(4 + 3) + 2 =$ _____

8 $(5 \times 4) \times 3 =$ _____

9 $7 + (15 + 2) =$ _____

A $4 + (3 + 2)$

B $4 \times 3 + 2$

C $4 + (3 + 1)$

D $7 + 2 + 3$

F $5 \times (4 \times 2)$

G $4 \times (5 \times 3)$

H 54×3

J none of the above

A $(7 + 5) + 12$

B $15 - 2 + 7$

C $(7 + 15) + 2$

D $71 + (5 + 2)$

Fill in the blanks.

10 The _____ property states that the way factors are grouped in multiplication does not change the product.

11 The associative property states that the way addends are _____ in addition does not change the _____.

12 Damon has 7 red T-shirts, 6 green T-shirts, and 15 white T-shirts. How many T-shirts does he have? Show three different ways to solve the problem.

_____

_____

_____

Short Response Question

13 Pam's mother teaches piano lessons 5 days a week. She teaches 5 lessons each day. How many lessons does she give in 6 weeks? Show at least 2 ways to solve the problem. What property did you use?

_____

_____

_____

Directions
Use a separate piece of paper to show your work.

1
$$541 \atop + \, 283$$

A 824
B 814
C 724
D None of these

2 $4 \times 124 =$

F 496
G 488
H 1,860
J None of these

3 $2 \times 6 =$ ____

$6 \times$ ____ $= 12$

4 $3 \times 5 =$ ____

____ + ____ + ____ = 15

5 8 boys like softball, 4 like tennis, and 7 like golf. 7 girls like softball, 8 like tennis, and 2 like golf. Complete the table including the totals.

Favorite Sports	Softball	Tennis	Golf
Boys	8		7
Girls	7	8	
Total			

6 Mike has 8 marbles. Ken has 7 marbles. Jill has 12 marbles. Does it matter what order they use to find the total number of marbles? Explain.

Answer _____

_____

7 Four classes sold 160 tickets to the school play. Grades 1 and 2 sold 40 tickets each. Grade 3 sold 20 tickets. How many tickets did Grade 4 sell?

Answer _____

_____

8 Nicole has 3 boxes of sports cards with 30 cards in each box. She gave 4 cards to a friend. How many cards does Nicole have left now?

Answer _____

_____

9 ◆ Ramon has 9 muffins for 3 of his friends. How many will each of them receive if he divides them equally?

A 2
B 3
C 9
D 1

10 Four students were chosen to give 5-minute speeches. Which of the following number sentences could **not** be used to find the total number of minutes?

F $5 + 5 + 5 + 5 =$ ____
G $4 \times 5 =$ ____
H $5 \times 4 =$ ____
J $4 + 4 + 4 + 4 + 4 =$ ____

Lesson 4.1 ▪ Properties of plane figures

> **READY REFERENCE**
> **plane** a flat surface that continues in all directions
> **plane figure** a geometric figure on a flat surface
> **line** a straight set of points that goes on forever with no endpoints
> **line segment** a part of a line with two endpoints
> **ray** a part of a line with one endpoint that goes on forever in one direction
> **angle** two rays with the same endpoint
> **vertex** the endpoint of an angle; the point where 3 or more edges meet
> **point** an exact location in space

Think About It

Geometry is all around us. Everywhere you look you see plane figures such as stop signs and buttons. How can you describe points, lines, line segments, rays, and angles?

Here's How

Points in a plane	Line
Label each point with a letter from the alphabet. Use A, B, and Y. • • • Read: point A, point ___, point Y. Write: A, B, ___.	Label the two points on the line with alphabet letters. For this exercise, use P and Q ←————————→ Read: line PQ **or** line QP. Write: $\overleftrightarrow{PQ}$ **or** $\overleftrightarrow{QP}$
Line segment	**Ray**
Label the two endpoints with alphabet letters. For this exercise, use R and M. •————————• Read: line segment _____ or line segment RM. Write: $\overline{RM}$ **or** $\overline{MR}$	Label the endpoint and one other point on each ray. For this exercise, use E and G, with E at the endpoint. •————————→ Read: ray EG. Always read the endpoint first. Write: $\overrightarrow{EG}$

Angle

Label the endpoint and one other point on the ray.
For this exercise, use X, Y, and Z, with X at the endpoint.

Read: angle X or angle YXZ or angle ZXY. The vertex is always the middle letter when you use three letters.

Write: ∠X or ∠YXZ or ∠ZXY

 Practice

Draw and label an example of each.

1 ∠QRZ   **2** $\overline{AB}$ **3** $\overrightarrow{FM}$ **4** $\overleftrightarrow{TS}$

Use symbols to name each figure.

5 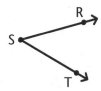   **6**    **7**    **8**

_____   _____   _____   _____

How would you read each of the following?

9 ∠PQR   **10** $\overline{NM}$ **11** $\overleftrightarrow{KL}$

_____   _____   _____

Short Response Question

12 Mary says that the following is angle M. Annie says it is angle PJM. Who is correct? Explain your answer.

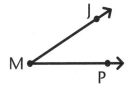

_____

_____

_____

Lesson 4.2 ▪ Properties of solid figures

> **READY REFERENCE**
>
> **solid figure** a three-dimensional solid shape that has length, width, and height; a space figure
>
> **edge** the segment where two faces of a space figure meet
>
> **face** a flat surface surrounded by line segments
>
> **vertex** the point where 3 or more edges meet in a solid figure; the plural is vertices

🔑 Think About It

Solid figures are not flat. The world is filled with solid objects, such as cereal boxes, paint cans, and ice cream cones. Vertices, faces, and edges describe parts of solid figures.

🔑 Here's How

Cube

A cube has 8 vertices, ____ faces, and 12 edges. All the faces of a cube are squares.

Rectangular Prism

A rectangular prism has ____ vertices, 6 faces, and ____ edges.

Pyramid

Pyramid A has ____ faces, ____ vertices, and ____ edges. All the faces are triangles. The base is a _____.
Pyramid B is a square pyramid. It has 5 faces, ____ edges, and ____ vertices. The base is a _____.

Cylinder

A cylinder has 0 edges, 0 faces, and 0 vertices. It has ____ flat surfaces. The flat surfaces are _____.

Cone

A cone has ____ flat surface shaped like a circle.

Sphere

A sphere has ____ flat surfaces.

🔑 Practice

Write the term for each solid figure.

1

2

3

4

_____

5

6

7

8

_____

How many faces, edges, and vertices does each figure have?

9

___ faces
___ edges
___ vertices

10

___ faces
___ edges
___ vertices

11

___ faces
___ edges
___ vertices

Short Response Question

12 How are a cube and a rectangular prism alike? How are they different?

_____

_____

_____

_____

Lesson 4.3 ▪ Designs and patterns with geometric figures

READY REFERENCE

pattern a set of actions that is repeated and does not change

flip a movement of a figure over a line that gives a mirror image

slide a movement of a figure along a line (up, down, or over)

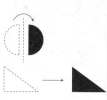

🔑 Think About It

Lay a book on your desk. Now "flip" the book as shown in the diagram. Is the book still the same size and shape?

You can use slides and flips to construct shapes and make patterns. When you use slides and flips, the size and shape of the figures do not change. In other words, the shapes remain congruent—they keep the same shape and size.

🔑 Here's How

Using flips and slides in patterns

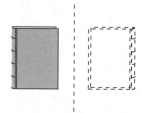

_____ _____ _____ _____

1. Are the figures similar? _____ Explain your answer.

   _____

2. Are the figures congruent? _____ How do you know?

   _____

3. Is the pattern a slide pattern or a flip pattern? It is a _____ pattern because it moves along a _____.

4. Complete the pattern.

Practice

Write slide *or* flip *under each pattern.*

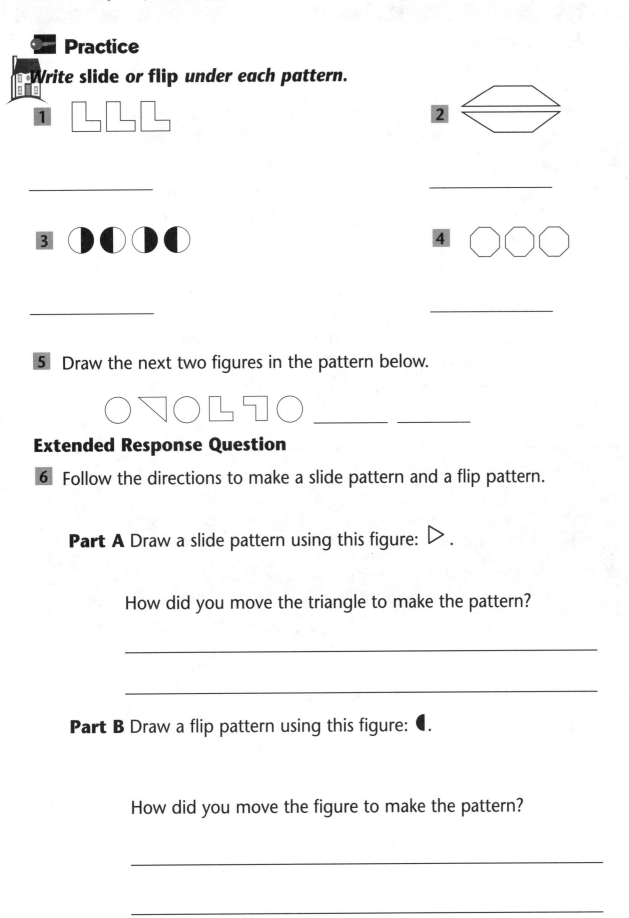

1 L L L

_____

2 ⬡

_____

3 ◐ ◐ ◐ ◐

_____

4 ⬡ ⬡ ⬡

_____

5 Draw the next two figures in the pattern below.

○ ◣ ○ └ ┐ ○ _____ _____

Extended Response Question

6 Follow the directions to make a slide pattern and a flip pattern.

Part A Draw a slide pattern using this figure: ▷ .

How did you move the triangle to make the pattern?

_____

_____

Part B Draw a flip pattern using this figure: ◖.

How did you move the figure to make the pattern?

_____

_____

Lesson 4.4 ▪ Ordered pairs on a grid

> **READY REFERENCE**
> **ordered pairs** a pair of numbers used to tell where to plot points on a grid

 **Think About It**

A grid is a kind of map. You can find your way around the grid using pairs of numbers called ordered pairs. An ordered pair can be used to find the location of a point on a grid.

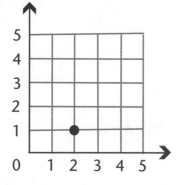

Ordered Pairs
Point *A*: (2, 1)
Point *B*: (4, 1)
Point *C*: (5, 3)
Point *D*: (3, 5)
Point *E*: (1, 3)

Here's How

Plot the ordered pairs.

1. The order of the numbers in an ordered pair is important. The first number tells you to move to the right. The second number tells you to move up. Point (1, 2) is at a different location than point (2, 1).

2. To plot point *A* (2, 1), start at 0 and move 2 squares to the right. Now move up 1 square. Place a point at that location and label the point *A*.

3. Plot point *B* (4, 1). Move 4 squares to the right and up 1 square.

4. Plot point C (5, 3). Move _____ squares to the right and up 3 squares.

5. Plot point *D* (3, 5). Move _____ squares to the right and up _____ squares.

6. Plot point *E* (1, 3). Move _____ square to the right and up _____ squares.

7. Draw lines to connect the points you have plotted. You should see a five-sided shape called a pentagon.

🔑 Practice

Use the grid to answer Problems 1–7.

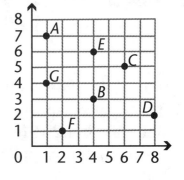

1 Point A is located at _____. Circle the correct letter.

  A (7, 1)   **B** (1, 7)   **C** (2, 6)   **D** (2, 7)

2 What point is located at (6, 5)?

_____

3 What point is located at (2, 1)?

_____

Write the ordered pair for each point.

4 point B _____   **5** point G _____   **6** point E _____   **7** point D _____

Short Response Question

8 **Use Grid 1 and Grid 2 to answer the questions.**

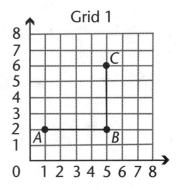

Grid 1

Part A Name the ordered pair (point D) you should plot in Grid 1 to complete the figure as a square. _____ Explain how you know.

_____

_____

Part B Plot point A, point B, and point C on Grid 2 to form a triangle. Which ordered pairs did you use?

  point A _____   point B _____   point C _____

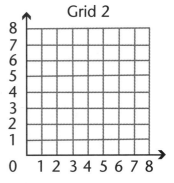

Grid 2

Lesson 4.5 ▪ Graphs and charts of real-world data

🔑 Think About It

The Appalachian Mountain chain has mountains of many different heights. Slide Mountain is 4,204 feet high, Mount Marcy is 5,344 feet high, Spruce Knob is 4,862 feet high, and High Point is 1,803 feet high. How would you construct a chart to display this data?

🔑 Here's How

1. Draw a chart below with 5 rows. In the top row, label the first column "Mountain." Label the second column "Height." What would be a good title for the chart? Give the chart a title.

2. What information should you write in the rows under "Mountain"? _____ Fill in the information, beginning with the tallest mountain and ending with the shortest mountain. Write the height of each mountain next to its name. (Make sure you have listed the mountains from tallest to shortest.)

🔑 Practice

1 Use the data in the chart to complete the bar graph.

Rainfall During Vacation

Day	Rainfall in Millimeters
Monday	8
Tuesday	6
Wednesday	0
Thursday	4
Friday	10

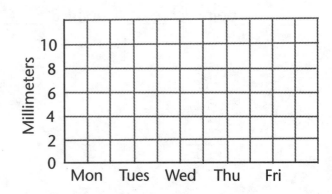

2 Complete the chart using the following data. Mrs. Vail's class has 15 boys and 5 girls. Mr. LaValle's class has 12 boys and 12 girls. Mr. Finn's class has 14 boys and 8 girls.

Class	Boys	Girls

3 The average rainfall in a year for New York City is almost 43 inches. The average rainfall in a year for Newark is a little more than 42 inches. The average rainfall in a year for Atlantic City is a little less than 42 inches. Use this data to label the graph and draw the bars.

40

4 Gina wants to use a circle graph to show the percentage of students in grades 1 – 4. Each grade contains 25% of the total number of students. Complete the circle graph using this information.

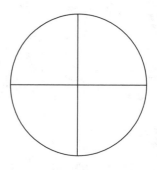

Short Response Question

5 Yesterday it rained 10 inches in New York City, 5 inches in Buffalo, 15 inches in Albany, and $2\frac{1}{2}$ inches in Rochester. Organize the data in a chart and make a bar graph using the data. Which is more helpful to you, the chart or the bar graph? _____ Explain your answer.

_____

_____

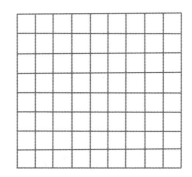

Lesson 4.6 ▪ Draw conclusions and make predictions from graphs

🔑 Think About It

Graphs can help us draw conclusions and make predictions. Thinking about the information in graphs can help you understand the data and make predictions about other things that might happen.

🔑 Here's How

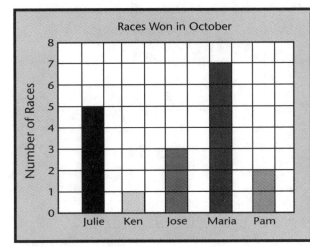

1. Who won the greatest number of races?
   _____

2. Who won the least number of races?
   _____

3. Who do you predict will win the next race? _____

4. Who do you predict will come in second in the next race? _____

🔑 Practice

1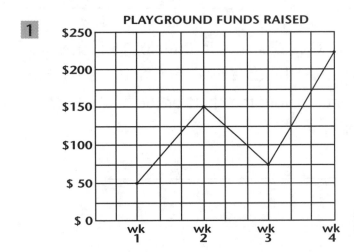

How much money was raised by the end of Week 4? _____ Show your work.

The school wants to buy a new piece of playground equipment for $550. There are 2 more weeks to raise funds. Do you think they will have enough money? _____ Why or why not?

_____

_____

_____

2

Science Fair Attendance

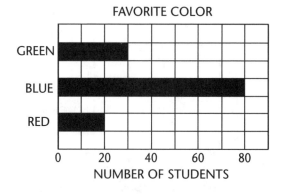

Thurs	𝟅 𝟅 𝟅
Fri	𝟅 𝟅 𝟅 𝟅
Sat	𝟅 𝟅 𝟅 𝟅 𝟅 𝟅
Each 𝟅 stands for 20 people.	

The science fair attendance has been the same for the past two years. What day next year do you think the most people will attend the fair?

_____

3

FAVORITE COLOR

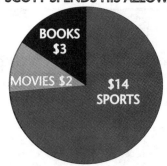

The fourth grade voted on their favorite color. How many students voted for green? _____ blue? _____ red? _____ What color had the most votes? _____ What color had the fewest votes? _____ What color uniforms do you think the students might vote for?

_____

4

HOW SCOTT SPENDS HIS ALLOWANCE

BOOKS $3

MOVIES $2

$14 SPORTS

How much money does Scott spend on books? _____ movies? _____ sports? _____ What do you think Scott's favorite activity is?

_____

Short Response Question

5 Plot the following data on the graph by plotting a point for each test score. Jennifer received the following test scores: Week 1, 75; Week 2, 85; Week 3, 90; Week 4, 95. Use your ruler to connect the points. Do you predict her score for Week 5 will go up or go down? _____ Explain your answer.

JENNIFER'S TEST SCORES

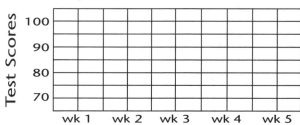

Test Scores

100
90
80
70

wk 1   wk 2   wk 3   wk 4   wk 5

_____

_____

_____

Lesson 4.7 ▪ Find perimeter, area, and volume by counting units

 Think About It

You can count units to find the perimeter, area, and volume of a plane figure or a space figure.

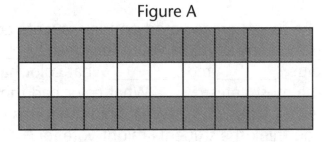

Figure A

Figure B

height

width

length

 Here's How

Find the perimeter of a plane figure.

Look at Figure A. The perimeter of the plane figure is the distance around the outside. Count the number of units all the way around the figure. The perimeter is _____ units.

Find the area of a plane figure.

Look at Figure A. The area of a plane figure is the number of square units that cover the surface. Count the number of square units that cover the surface. The area is _____ square units.

Find the volume of a space figure.

Look at Figure B. The volume of a space figure is the number of cubic units that fit inside the figure.

1. Count the number of unit cubes in each row to find the length. Length = _____

2. Count the number of rows to find the width. Width = _____

3. Count the number of layers in the figure to find the height. Height = _____

4. What is the total number of unit cubes in the figure?

    Volume = _____

Practice

Use Figure C to answer Problems 1–2. Show your work.

1 What is the perimeter of Figure C? _____   **2** What is the area of Figure C? _____

Find the volume in Problems 3–4.

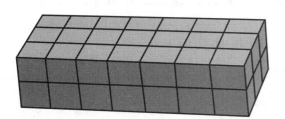

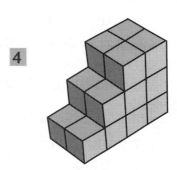

_____   _____

Short Response Question

5 *Explain how you found the area and the volume for the shape below.*

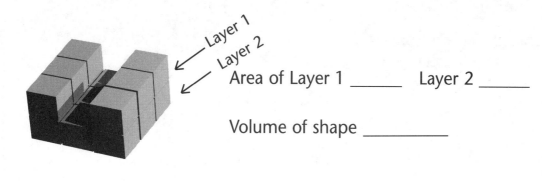

Area of Layer 1 _____   Layer 2 _____

Volume of shape _____

_____

_____

_____

_____

Lesson 4.8 ▪ Find the circumference of circles by measuring with string

READY REFERENCE

circumference the distance around a circle

diameter a line segment that passes through the center of a circle with both endpoints on the circle

radius a line segment that has one endpoint on the center of a circle and one endpoint on the circle

 Think About It

You can measure the circumference of a circle with a piece of string. The circumference of a circle is about 3 times the diameter of a circle, so if you know the circumference you can estimate the diameter by dividing by 3. If you know the diameter, you can estimate the circumference by multiplying by 3.

The radius is $\frac{1}{2}$ the length of the diameter. If you know the diameter, divide by 2 to find the radius. Multiply the radius by 2 to find the length of the diameter.

 Here's How

Step 1 Place a piece of string around the circumference of the circle.

Step 2 Mark the string or cut it to fit around the circle.

Step 3 Measure the string to find the circumference of the circle. What is the circumference of the circle? _____

Step 4 To estimate the diameter of the circle, divide the circumference by 3. The diameter of the circle is about _____ cm.

Step 5 To estimate the radius of the circle, divide the diameter by 2. The radius of the circle is about _____ cm.

Practice

The circumferences of four circles are shown below in Problems 1–4. Estimate the diameter and the radius for each circle.

1

| 0 1 2 3 4 5 6 7 8 9 10 11 12 |
| centimeter |

circumference _____cm

diameter _____cm

radius _____cm

2

| 0 1 2 3 4 5 6 7 8 |
| inches |

circumference _____in

diameter _____in

radius _____in

3

| 0 1 2 3 4 5 6 7 8 9 10 11 12 |
| centimeter |

circumference _____cm

diameter _____cm

radius _____cm

4

| 0 1 2 3 4 5 6 7 8 |
| inches |

circumference _____in

diameter _____in

radius _____in

Short Response Question

5 Use a piece of string to measure the circumference of the circle. Use the measured string to estimate the diameter and the radius. Explain how you estimated the diameter and the radius.

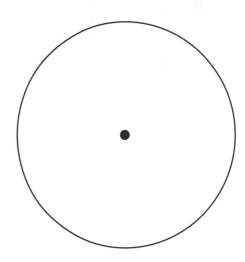

circumference _____cm

diameter _____cm

radius _____cm

_____

_____

_____

Lesson 4.9 ▪ Find the area of circles by counting units in a grid

 Think About It

You know that area is the number of square units needed to cover a flat surface. How do you estimate the area of a circle?

Here's How

Step 1	Count the number of whole units that are inside the circle. There are _____ square units inside the circle.	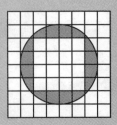
Step 2	Count the number of shaded units inside the circle that are not whole squares. There are about _____ shaded shapes.	
Step 3	Add the number of square units from Step 1 and Step 2. The estimated area of the circle is about _____ square units.	

Practice

Estimate the area for the circles in Problems 1–4. Show your work.

1

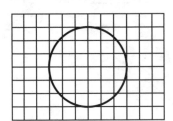

area _____

2

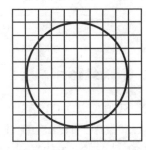

area _____

3

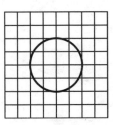

area _____

4

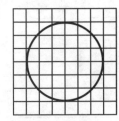

area _____

Circle the letter for the estimated area for Problems 5–6.

5

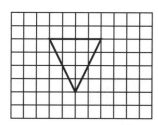

A 4   **C** 8

B 13   **D** 3

6

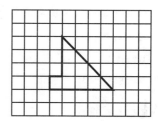

F 9   **H** 4

G 7   **J** 12

Short Response Question

7 Can you estimate the area for Figures A, B, and C by using the same method you used for estimating the area of a circle? Explain why or why not.

A

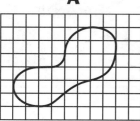

B

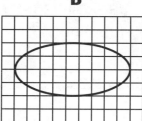

C

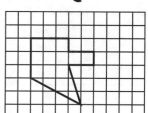

_____

_____

_____

_____

Lesson 4.10 ▪ Understanding volume by filling space

> **READY REFERENCE**
> **volume** the number of cubic units a space figure contains

 Think About It

To find the volume of a space figure, you can build the space figure with connecting cubes and then count the cubes that it took to build the figure. How many cubic units will it take to fill up this figure? If you know how many cubic units fill up the figure, you know the volume of the figure.

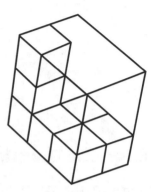

 Here's How

Step 1 Use connecting cubes to build the figure.

Step 2 Count the cubes that you used to build the figure. _____ The volume of the figure is the same as the number of cubes it takes to fill up the figure.

Volume = _____ cubic units

 Practice

Use connecting cubes to build the following shapes. Count the cubes to find the volume.

1

volume = _____ cubic units

2

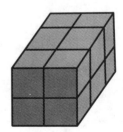

volume = _____ cubic units

3

volume = _____ cubic units

4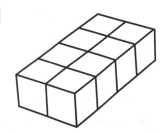

volume = _____ cubic units

 5 Nicolas has 8 connecting cubes. Christopher has 5 connecting cubes. Do they each have enough cubes to build the space figure? _____

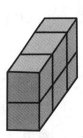

Short Response Question

6 Look at the figure. How many figures can you build if you have 24 connecting cubes? _____ Explain your answer.

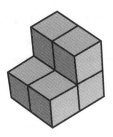

_____

_____

_____

_____

Lesson 4.11 ▪ Compare temperatures and heights over time

🔑 Think About It

You know that you are growing. The clothes you have now probably won't fit you in a year. Can you predict how much you will grow over the next 6 months?

🔑 Here's How

Collier is 48 inches tall. He has been measuring his height for 4 months. Each month he has grown about $\frac{1}{4}$ of an inch. If he continues growing at this rate, how tall will he be when summer comes?

Look at the chart Collier made. It shows his height for each of the 4 months.

Add $\frac{1}{4}$ inch to each month. Write the predicted height on the line.

October	$47\frac{1}{4}$ inches
November	$47\frac{1}{2}$ inches
December	$47\frac{3}{4}$ inches
January	48 inches
February	
March	
April	
May	
June	

1. How tall will Collier be in June? _____

2. How tall will he be in April? _____

🔑 Practice

1. The high temperature of the day drops one degree every day in October. If the high temperature on October 1 is 68 degrees, predict the high temperature for October 20. _____ Make a chart that shows how you got your answer.

2 Corbin and Monica gather apples from the orchard. Every day they pick 5 more apples than they did the day before. If they start on September 5 by picking 15 apples, how many will they pick on September 13?

_____ Make a chart that shows how you got your answer.

3 Chase knew that he was growing quickly. He gained $\frac{1}{2}$ pound last month and $\frac{1}{2}$ pound this month. He now weighs 55 pounds. If he grows at the same rate, how much will he weigh in 2 months? _____ If he gains only $\frac{1}{4}$ pound each month, how much will he weigh in 2 months? _____ Make a chart for each of Chase's growth possibilities.

Short Response Question

4 Measure your height. If you were to grow $\frac{1}{4}$ inch every month, how tall would you be in six months? _____ Make a chart to show your predicted growth.

Describe how you calculated your height.

_____

_____

_____

Lesson 4.12 ▪ Geometric terms

READY REFERENCE

polygon a plane figure made up of 3 or more line segments

chord a line segment with both of its endpoints on a circle

radius a line segment with one endpoint in the center of a circle and the other endpoint on the circle

face a flat surface of a space figure

edge the segment where two faces of a space figure meet

vertex the point where 2 sides of a polygon or 3 edges of a space figure meet

angle formed by two rays with the same endpoint

line segment a part of a line with 2 endpoints

point an exact location in space

parallel lines lines in the same plane that never intersect

perpendicular lines two lines that intersect and form 4 right angles

intersecting lines lines that have 1 point in common

 Think About It

There are words or terms that describe ideas in geometry. People use these terms when they talk about the shapes.

 Here's How

To understand the terms in geometry, you must know what they look like as well as remember the terms. Look at the following examples.

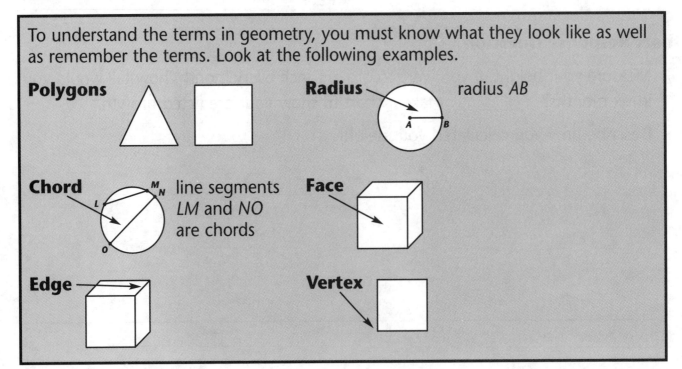

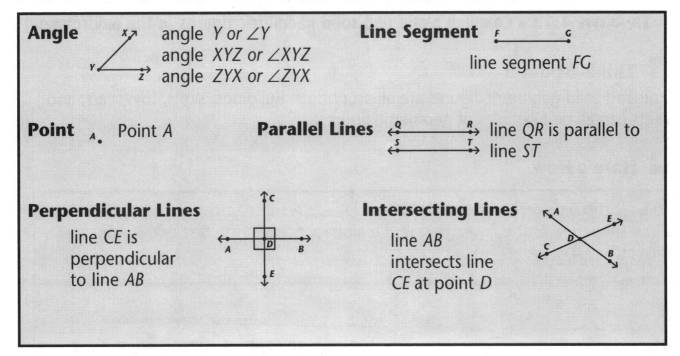

Angle angle *Y* or ∠*Y* angle *XYZ* or ∠*XYZ* angle *ZYX* or ∠*ZYX*	**Line Segment** line segment *FG*
Point Point *A*	**Parallel Lines** line *QR* is parallel to line *ST*
Perpendicular Lines line *CE* is perpendicular to line *AB*	**Intersecting Lines** line *AB* intersects line *CE* at point *D*

Practice

1 **Circle the figures that are polygons.**

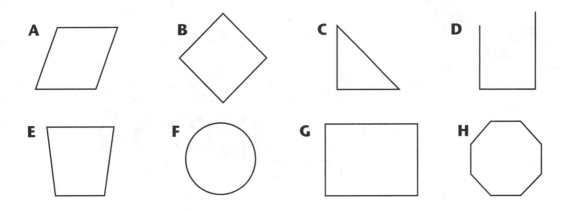

A B C D

E F G H

Short Response Question

2 On the lines below, explain why the figures you chose are polygons and the others are not polygons.

_____

_____

_____

_____

Lesson 4.13 • Common plane and solid geometric figures in the environment

Think About It

Plane and solid geometric figures are all around us. Buildings, signs, toys, cars, and streets can all be examples of geometric figures.

Here's How

Look at the picture. There is an alphabet letter on some of the geometric figures. Write the name of the figure beside the alphabet letter. The first one is done for you.

A sphere _____   E _____

B _____   F _____

C _____   G _____

D _____   H _____

Practice

Underline the correct term for each figure.

1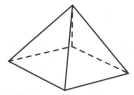

cone
square pyramid
sphere

2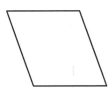

hexagon
square
parallelogram

3

sphere
cylinder
cone

4

square
cylinder
rectangle

5

rectangle
square
circle

6

cone
cylinder
square

7

cone
square pyramid
cube

8

rectangular prism
circle
parallelogram

9

cylinder
sphere
rectangular prism

Short Response Question

 10 On the lines below, list the geometric figures you see in your classroom and the names of those figures. An example is done for you. On a separate sheet of paper, make a list of geometric figures you see at home.

The clock is a circle. _____   _____

_____   _____   _____

_____   _____   _____

Lesson 4.14 ▪ Using rulers, protractors, and compasses

 Think About It

You can draw all sorts of geometric figures by using a few simple tools.

Here's How

Using a ruler.

1. How long is the side? _____

2. Use a ruler and draw a square to the right of the square above. Be sure to make your square measure the same length on the sides as the one pictured.

Using a compass.

3. What is the radius of the circle? _____

4. Use a compass to draw a circle to the right of the circle above. Be sure to make your radius the same length as the one in the circle pictured.

5. Draw in the radius on the circle you made. Label its length.

Use a protractor.

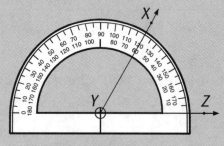

∠XYZ measures 60°

6. Angle XYZ measures 60°. Use a protractor to draw an angle that measures 80°.

⚷ Practice

Draw the figures using the measurements given.

1 Circle with a radius of $\frac{1}{2}$ in

2 Rectangle with sides of $1\frac{1}{2}$ in and 1 in

3 Two parallel lines, each $1\frac{3}{4}$ in long

4 Parallelogram with one side 2 in and the other side $\frac{1}{2}$ in

5 Line segment 2 in long

6 Ray $1\frac{1}{4}$ in long

7 Square with sides of $1\frac{1}{2}$ in

8 Two intersecting line segments: one is 1 in long, the other is $1\frac{1}{2}$ in long

9 Angle that is 50°

Short Response Question

 10 On the lines below, write the names of three geometric figures you see in your classroom. Then measure each figure and write its measurements on the line to the right.

Object   Measurement

_____   _____

_____   _____

_____   _____

Lesson 4.15 ▪ Lines of symmetry

> **READY REFERENCE**
> **symmetry** a figure has symmetry if it can be folded on a line so that the two parts match each other perfectly.

 Think About It

How do you know if a figure has lines of symmetry?

 Here's How

Look at the figure below. Notice the dotted line that divides the figure in two.

 Are the two parts equal? If they are equal, or match exactly, they are symmetrical. The line that divides the 2 parts is called a line of symmetry.

1. Can a line of symmetry be drawn on this figure? _____ Draw the line of symmetry.

2. Can a line of symmetry be drawn on this figure? _____ Draw the line of symmetry.

3. Can a line of symmetry be drawn on this figure? _____ Draw the line of symmetry.

 Practice

Draw a line of symmetry for each of the figures below. If a line cannot be drawn, write Not symmetrical *under the figure.*

1

2

3

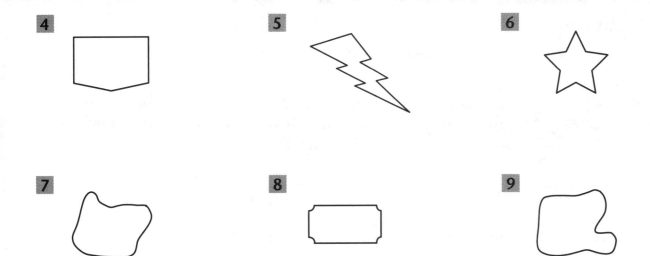

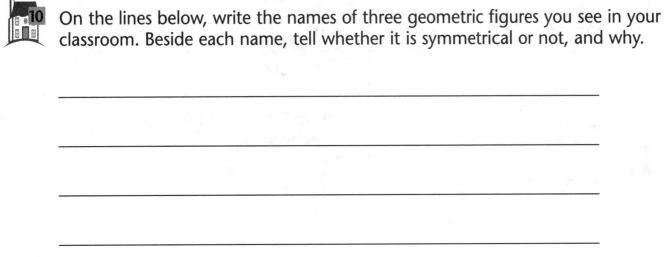

Short Response Question

10 On the lines below, write the names of three geometric figures you see in your classroom. Beside each name, tell whether it is symmetrical or not, and why.

_____

_____

_____

_____

Directions

Use a separate piece of paper to show your work.

1 How many faces, edges, and vertices does this figure have?

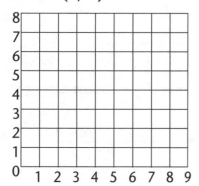

A 4 faces, 6 edges, 4 vertices
B 6 faces, 8 edges, 6 vertices
C 6 faces, 12 edges, 8 vertices
D 8 faces, 8 edges, 8 vertices

2 Plot the ordered pairs on the grid.

Point *A:* (2, 1)
Point *B:* (6, 1)
Point *C:* (6, 5)

3 If you connect the points in the grid in Problem 2, what geometric plane figure do you see?

F rectangle
G square pyramid
H triangle
J parallelogram

4 According to the chart below, in which year did the fourth grade have the most race winners?

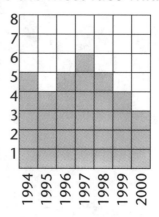

A 1995
B 1997
C 1998
D 2000

5 Which line segments are perpendicular?

F
G
H
J

6 Use your compass to draw a circle with a diameter of 2 in. Draw the radius of the circle.

Lesson 5.1 ▪ Choosing the correct metric units

READY REFERENCE

length the distance between two points

perimeter the distance around the sides of a polygon

weight or mass the amount of matter that an object contains; the heaviness of an object

capacity the amount a container can hold

area the number of square units needed to cover a flat surface

volume the number of cubic units that fit inside a space figure

🔑 Think About It

Did you know? A large paper clip is about 1 centimeter (1 cm) wide. A baseball bat is about 1 meter (1 m) long. There are about 20 drops of water in 1 milliliter (1 mL). A bottle of soda holds 1 liter (1 L). How would you measure these objects? What metric measurements would you use?

Area of a tabletop	Capacity of an aquarium	Perimeter of a computer monitor
Mass of a textbook	Volume of a shoe box	

🔑 Here's How

A mysterious box is delivered to your house. A secret message is attached to the top. The secret message says you will find fame and fortune if you can answer the questions. Tell your teacher or another student how you decided on the answers.

Step 1 Think about what you are being asked to discover. Is it length, weight, perimeter, or something else?

1. If you use kilograms, you would be finding the _____.

2. If you use square centimeters, are you finding area or volume? _____

3. If you use meters, you might be finding _____ or _____.

Step 2 Decide what type of measurement to use.

4. The secret message says to find the volume. Name two types of metric units of measure you could use. _____

5. The secret message says to find the perimeter. Name one type of English measure and two types of metric units of measure you could use. _____

Practice

Read the descriptions below. Decide if the characteristic being measured is length, perimeter, mass, capacity, area, or volume. Write the name of the characteristic on the line.

_____ **1** This box will hold five cubic meters of packing peanuts.

_____ **2** I need a pint of cream to finish this recipe.

_____ **3** My cookies are very healthy because each one has only three milligrams of fat.

_____ **4** The state of New York covers 47,224 square miles of land.

_____ **5** It is 415 km from Albany, New York, to Buffalo, New York.

_____ **6** That playground measures 122 meters around the sides.

_____ **7** That thermos holds 2 liters of my favorite juice.

_____ **8** The Adirondack Mountains rise to 1,630 meters above sea level.

Answer the following. Circle the letter of the best estimate.

9 Length of a soccer field   **A** 100 cm   **B** 100 m   **C** 10 m   **D** 10 cm

10 Length of a bed   **F** 20 cm   **G** 200 m   **H** 2 cm   **J** 2 m

11 Height of a dog   **A** 20 cm   **B** 1 m   **C** 10 m   **D** 5,000 cm

12 Look at the bottle of soda. Estimate whether each item holds *more* or *less* than 1 liter. Write *more* or *less* on the line.

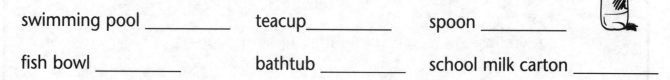

swimming pool _____   teacup_____   spoon _____

fish bowl _____   bathtub _____   school milk carton _____

Short Response Question

13 Explain how you estimated whether a teacup holds less than or more than 1 liter.

_____

_____

Lesson 5.2 ▪ Equivalent metric units

> **READY REFERENCE**
>
> | Length | Mass/Weight |
> |---|---|
>
> **Length**
> 10 millimeters (mm) = 1 centimeter (cm)
> 100 millimeters (mm) = 1 decimeter (dm)
> 1 decimeter (dm) = 10 centimeters (cm)
> 1 meter (m) = 100 centimeters
> 1 kilometer (km) = 1,000 meters
>
> **Mass/Weight**
> 1 kilogram (kg) = 1,000 grams (g)
>
> **Capacity**
> 1 liter (L) = 1,000 milliliters (mL)

🔑 Think About It

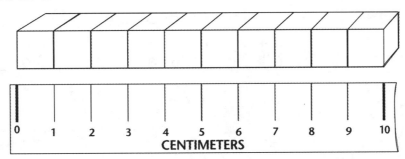

Use your ruler or look at this ruler. How long is this metric ruler? Use your base-10 blocks. If you place a tens rod above the ruler, you can see that a tens rod is about 1 decimeter long. How many centimeters are in a decimeter? Measure your pencil using your metric ruler. To the nearest centimeter, how long is the pencil? To the nearest decimeter, how long is the pencil? Look at your shoe and estimate the length of your shoe to the nearest centimeter and decimeter. Is your shoe greater than or less than 5 centimeters? Is it greater than or less than 5 meters?

🔑 Here's How

Suppose you are in charge of cooking the turkeys for Thanksgiving dinner for your family and friends. You cook two turkeys. One turkey has a mass of 12,000 g. The second turkey has a mass of 15 kg. Which turkey has the greatest mass?

> **Step 1** Think about what units of measurement to use. Study the problem. Is 12,000 grams greater than or less than 15 kilograms?
>
> 1. Write the problem. 12,000 g _____ _____ kg
>
> 2. I know that _____ kilogram = _____ grams

Step 2 Compute to rename the units.

    3. Use multiplication.   15 kg = (_____ × 1,000 g)

                        15 kg = _____ g

                        12,000 g < _____ g

                        12,000 g _____ 15 kg

    4. Which turkey has the greatest mass? _____

 Practice

Compare the numbers. Write <, =, or > in the blanks.

1 7 kg ____ 8,000 g   **2** 7,000 g ____ 6 kg   **3** 60 g ____ 6 kg

4 9,000 mL ____ 10 L   **5** 17 L ____ 1,700 mL   **6** 3 L ____ 300 mL

7 60 km ____ 600 m   **8** 4,000 mm ____ 400 cm   **9** 9 dm ____ 9,000 mm

Read each problem carefully. Think about how to solve the problem. Write the problem in numbers and find the answer.

10 Mr. Burley's car uses 1 L of gasoline to drive 6 km. How much gasoline does Mr. Burley need to travel 60 kilometers? _____

11 Laurie is making lemonade for a picnic. She has a thermos that holds 4 L of liquid. The thermos has 350 mL of lemonade in it. How much more lemonade does Laurie need to fill the thermos? _____

Short Response Question

12 Roberto and Michael are measuring a wall in their tree house to decide what size table to build. Roberto measures the wall and says it is 41 decimeters long. Michael measures the wall and says it is 410 centimeters long. Can Roberto and Michael both be right? Show your work and explain your answer.

_____

_____

_____

Lesson 5.3 ▪ Decimals and metric measurement tools

READY REFERENCE

decimal a number in base 10 written with one or more places to the right of the decimal point

metric system a system of measurement based on multiples of 10 that uses centimeter, decimeter, meter, and kilometer; milliliters and liters; grams and kilograms; and measures temperature in Celsius

Metric Units of Measurement	Base-10 Blocks
1 meter = 100 centimeters	1 base-10 rod = 10 ones
1 meter = 10 decimeters	1 hundreds block = 100 ones
1 decimeter = 10 centimeters	1 hundreds block = 10 ten rods
1 centimeter = 10 millimeters	

Money	Decimals
1 dollar = 10 dimes	1 = 10 tenths
1 dime = 10 pennies	1 = 100 hundredths

🔑 Think About It

Close your eyes and picture the number 10. You are walking down the street and find a penny. You pick it up and think, "If I had 10 pennies, I'd have a dime. If I had 10 dimes, I'd have a dollar. If I had 10 dollars, I could trade them for a ten dollar bill. If I had 10 ten dollar bills, I could trade them for a one hundred dollar bill!" How is that like a meter stick or base-10 blocks?

🔑 Here's How

How are decimals and the metric system related? They are both based on the number 10. Look at this metric ruler.

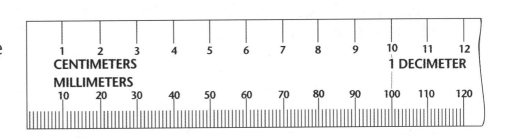

1. What metric units of measure do you see on this ruler? Write the units of measurement from smallest to largest. _____

2. The smallest unit of measurement on the ruler is _____ _____.
   (number) (unit of measurement)

3. One group of 10 milliliters = _____ _____.
   (number) (unit of measurement)

4. 10 _____ = _____ decimeter

5. _____ _____ = 1 meter

6. Read 1–5 again to yourself. Is this statement true or false?
   10 of one unit = 1 of the next largest unit. _____

Use your metric ruler.

1. Measure your hand. Complete this sentence. My hand measures about
   _____ decimeters.

2. Find something in your classroom that is about 1 meter long. It might be a
   backpack, several books, a chair, a coat, or something else. You will use this to
   estimate length in meters. You can call this your "meter estimator." What will
   you use? _____

Practice

1. Measure the length of your classroom. Should you use your hand or your meter
   estimator? Which would be faster? _____ Complete this sentence.
   My classroom is approximately _____ meters long.

2. Look at the top of your desk. Should you use decimeters or meters to measure it?
   _____ Should you use your hand or your meter estimator to
   measure the length and width of the top of your desk? Complete these sentences.
   My desk is approximately _____ _____ long. My desk is
   approximately _____ _____ wide.

Choose the best estimate.

3. A skateboard measures about   **A** 700 cm   **B** 7,000 cm   **C** 7 cm   **D** 70 cm

4. A fingernail measures about   **F** 1 m   **G** 1 cm   **H** 1 mm   **J** 1 dm

Short Response Question

5. Think about what you could measure at home with your hand. Does it make more
   sense to measure your living room with your hand or your meter estimator?
   _____ Name two things you could measure at home and tell what
   you could use to measure them. _____

Lesson 5.4 ▪ Clocks and fractions of a circle

READY REFERENCE

fraction a number that names part of a whole unit
equivalent fractions fractions that name the same amount; example: $\frac{1}{2}$ and $\frac{2}{4}$

🔑 Think About It

How can a clock help you understand fractions? Can you think of a way to use a clock to measure fractions of a circle? Picture a clock or look at the clock on your classroom wall. Most clocks are in the shape of a _____. If your answer is a circle, you are right. Have you ever used a circle to show fractions? Do you think you could use a clock to show fractions?

🔑 Here's How

1. This clock has no hands. The entire clock face looks like a circle. Do the circle and the clock show 1 or $\frac{1}{2}$?

   _____

2. The time on the clock shows _____.

3. What fraction does the shaded part of the clock show?

   _____

4. What fraction does the part that is not shaded show? _____

5. The circle is now divided into _____ parts.

6. Draw clock hands on the clock so it shows 4:00. Shade the part between the 12 and the 4. What fraction does the shaded part show? _____
   $\frac{4}{12}$ is the same as $\frac{1}{3}$.

🔑 Practice

Circle the letter of the correct answer.

1. Draw hands on the clock to show 8:25. Use your pencil to shade the space inside the hands. What equivalent fractions are represented by the shaded part of the clock?

   A $\frac{6}{12}, \frac{1}{2}$ **B** $\frac{3}{6}, \frac{12}{24}$ **C** $\frac{3}{12}, \frac{1}{4}$ **D** $\frac{4}{12}, \frac{1}{3}$

2. Draw hands on the clock to show 8:00. Use your pencil to shade the space inside the hands. What equivalent fractions are represented by the shaded part of the clock?

   F $\frac{4}{12}, \frac{1}{3}$ **G** $\frac{8}{12}, \frac{2}{3}$ **H** $\frac{3}{12}, \frac{1}{4}$ **J** $\frac{2}{12}, \frac{1}{6}$

3. Draw hands on the clock to show 2:30. Shade the space inside the hands. What fraction does the shaded part show? _____ Name an equivalent fraction for the shaded part. _____

4. Draw hands on the clock to show 8:20. Shade the entire clock **except** the space inside the hands. What fraction does the shaded part show? _____ Name an equivalent fraction for the shaded part. _____

5. Draw a clock. Now draw the hands to show 9:15. How many equivalent fractions can you name?

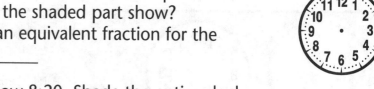

Short Response Question

6. 🏠 Tony spent $\frac{1}{3}$ of an hour writing a poem. Victoria spent $\frac{1}{4}$ of an hour writing a poem. Who spent more time writing? Show your work and explain your answer.

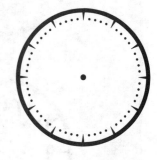

_____

_____

_____

Lesson 5.5 ▪ Minutes and seconds

> **READY REFERENCE**
> **minute** a unit of time that equals 60 seconds
> **second** a unit of time; 60 seconds equals 1 minute

🔑 Think About It

Can a person swim under water for one second? Can a person swim under water for one minute? Can a person swim under water for five minutes? Say "one thousand one." In the time it takes to say one thousand one, about one second has passed. If you counted from one thousand one all the way to one thousand sixty, it would take about 60 seconds or one minute. How far would you have to count for five minutes?

🔑 Here's How

The hour and the minute hands show 45 minutes after 5 o'clock, or 5:45.

The second hand shows 6 seconds after 5:45.

The time on the clock is five forty-five and six seconds.

1. The time on this clock is _____
   and _____ seconds.
2. Write the time in words. _____
3. Look at this clock and the one above. How many
   minutes have gone by? _____

4. The time on the clock is now _____ and
   _____ seconds.
5. How many minutes have gone by? _____

6. The time on the clock is now _____ and
   _____ seconds.
7. How many more seconds have gone by? _____

8. Write the time in words. _____

   _____

9:10

9. One minute goes by. The time would be _____.
   Draw the clock.

   _____

10. In five minutes, the time will be _____.

9:20

**Multiply to change from a larger unit of time
to a smaller unit of time. Solve this problem.** 7 minutes = _____ seconds

11. How many seconds in a minute?   1 minute = _____ seconds

                                     7 minutes = _____ × 60 seconds

                                     7 minutes = _____ seconds

🔑 Practice

Write each time two ways using numbers and words.

 1   **2**   **3**   **4**  3:33

_____   _____   _____   _____

_____   _____   _____   _____

Write each missing number.

5 6 min = _____ s   **6** 1 h = _____ min   **7** 1 h = _____ s

8 4 hr = _____ min   **9** 1 min 10 s = _____ s   **10** 6 h = _____ min

11 1 h 10 min = _____ min **12** 4 h 45 min = _____ min **13** 9 h 17 min = _____ min

Extended Response Question

14 The clock in your classroom loses 4 minutes each day. If the clock shows 9 A.M. on
Monday, what time will the clock show in 23 days? Show your work and explain
your answer.

_____

_____

Lesson 5.6 ▪ Area, volume, and counting units

READY REFERENCE

area the number of square units needed to cover a flat surface

volume the number of cubic units that fit inside a space figure

---

Think About It

You walk into your kitchen. There on the kitchen table is a jug of delicious lemonade and a box of cookies. There's a note from your mother that says, "I have a challenge for you. If you can find the area of the kitchen tabletop and the volume of the cookie box, you can help yourself to a glass of lemonade and three cookies." What do you need to know to find the area of the kitchen tabletop? What do you need to know to find the volume of the cookie box?

Here's How

Find the area by counting the square units.

1. There are _____ tiles in the tabletop.

2. The area of the tabletop is _____ square units.

Look at the dark tiles that form an irregular shape in the middle of the tabletop. What is the area of the irregular shape?

3. Count the square units to find the area of the irregular shape. Since each ■ is equal to 1 square unit, the area of the irregular shape is _____ square units.

4. Find the area of this irregular shape by counting whole units and half units and adding.

4 tiles wide

8 tiles long

Each ◎ = 1 square unit

Each ◿ = $\frac{1}{2}$ square unit

Find the volume by counting the unit cubes.

You can use unit cubes to make a model of the cookie box.

1. How many unit cubes are in each row? _____ This number is the length.

width

length

How many rows are there? _____
This number is the width. How many unit cubes
are in one layer? _____

2. I need _____ layers to finish the model
of the cookie box. This number is the height.

3. The total number of unit cubes needed to build
the model is _____ . This number is the volume.

Practice

Find the area in square units.

1 _____

2 _____

3 _____

4 _____

5 _____

6 _____

7 _____

8 _____

Find the volume of each space figure.

9 _____

10 _____

11 _____

12 _____

13 _____

14 _____

Short Response Question

15 Mr. Gonzalez bought 49 square tiles to cover a patio table. The surface of the
tabletop is the same number of units long as it is wide. Draw and describe the
shape of the surface.

_____

_____

Lesson 5.7 ▪ Area, volume, and multiplication

> **READY REFERENCE**
> **area** the number of square units needed to cover a flat surface
> **volume** the number of cubic units that fit inside a space figure

🔑 Think About It

You walk into your kitchen. There on the kitchen table is a jug of delicious lemonade and a plate of cookies. There's another note from your mother that says, "I have a new challenge for you today. If you can find the area of the kitchen tabletop and the volume of a box, you can help yourself to a glass of lemonade and three cookies. YOU MUST USE MULTIPLICATION TO SOLVE THIS PROBLEM!" What do you need to know to find the area of the kitchen tabletop? What do you need to know to find the volume of the box?

🔑 Here's How

Find the area by multiplying.

1. The tabletop is ____ feet wide.

2. The tabletop is ____ feet long.

3. To find the area, multiply length × width.

   Area = ____ × width

   Area = ____ feet × 4 feet = ____ square feet

(diagram: 4 ft. wide, 8 ft. long)

Find the volume by multiplying.

1. The box is ____ units high, ____ units long, and ____ units wide.

2. To find the volume, multiply the length by the width by the height.

   Volume = length × _____ × _____

   Volume = 8 m × ____ m × ____ m = ____ cubic meters

(diagram: 3 m height, 8 m length, 4 m width)

3. Look at each rectangular prism. Fill in the chart to calculate the volume.

	Length	Width	Height	Volume
Example	5 units	2 units	2 units	20 cubic units
Figure 1	5 units			
Figure 2		4 units		

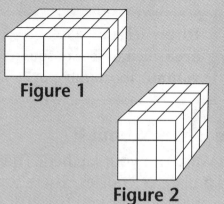

Figure 1

Figure 2

 **Practice**

Use multiplication to find the area in square units.

1 12 in.

2 37 cm

3 9 ft   17 ft

Use multiplication to find the volume of each space figure.

4 8 cm   8 cm   8 cm

5 4 yd   4 yd   22 yd

6 5 mm   5 mm   5 mm

7 Sandy would like to have new wall-to-wall carpeting in her bedroom. The carpet costs $2.00 a square foot. The room measures 11 ft by 13 ft. How much will the carpeting cost?

Short Response Question

8 There are 10 rows of unit cubes in each layer of a box. There are 10 cubes in each row. How many layers are there if there are 700 unit cubes in the box? Explain your answer.

_____

_____

Lesson 5.8 ▪ Measurement and the content areas

Think About It

What does measurement have to do with social studies, science, or literature? Have you ever thought about how math is related to other subjects? In *The Incredible Journey*, by Sheila Burnford, three runaway pets—a young Labrador retriever, a wise bull terrier, and a Siamese cat—help one another through hardships, hunger, and danger as they travel more than 200 miles through the Canadian wilderness to make their way home. How long might it have taken the animals to travel 200 miles if they traveled 5 miles a day?

Here's How

Step 1 Think about the problem. What do you already know?

    1. I know that the animals traveled a total of _____ miles. They could travel _____ miles in 1 day.

Step 2 Think about what you want to find out.

    2. I want to know _____.

Step 3 Set up the problem. Decide if you need to add, subtract, multiply, or divide.

    3. What should you do to find the number of days the journey took?

      A Subtract the number of miles traveled in 1 day from the total number of miles.

      B Divide the total number of miles by the number of miles traveled in 1 day.

      C Divide the number of miles traveled in 1 day by the total number of miles.

      D Add the total number of miles to the number of miles traveled in 1 day.

Step 4 Write the problem and calculate the answer.

🔑 Practice

1. The male bee hummingbird of Cuba is the world's smallest bird. Its wingspan is about 6 cm long. How many millimeters is the wingspan? _____

2. It is 104 kilometers from Binghamton to Cooperstown. The delivery truck drives from Binghamton to Cooperstown and back again to Binghamton every day. How many total kilometers will the truck travel if it makes the trip Monday through Friday? _____

3. A 1 L bottle of soda holds 3 servings. Each serving has 125 mL of sodium. How much sodium is in a 1 L bottle? How much sodium is in 21 servings? _____

4. Two towns decide to join together to form one city. Town A covers 15 square miles. Town B covers 9 square miles. How many square miles will the new city be? _____

Short Response Question

5. The endangered leatherback sea turtle can grow to a mass of 636 kg. The endangered black rhinoceros of Africa can reach 1,770 kg. How many kilograms more is the black rhinoceros? About how many leatherback sea turtles would equal the mass of a black rhinoceros? Show your work and explain your answer.

_____

_____

_____

Lesson 5.9 ▪ Select and use appropriate metric measurement tools

Think About It

Metersticks, metric rulers, Celsius thermometers, metric scales, and metric measuring cups are all metric measurement tools. How do you choose the correct measurement tool?

Here's How

Jessica wants to know if her desk will fit in her bedroom between the door and the closet. What metric measurement tool should she use to find out?

Step 1 Estimate the length of one of the items and choose an appropriate tool. Jessica estimates that the desk is 1 meter long, so she chooses a meter stick as her measuring tool.

Step 2 Measure the items with the measuring tool. Jessica measures the desk and then the space between the door and the closet with a meter stick.

Step 3 Compare the two measurements. The desk measurement cannot be longer than the space it must fit into.

Practice

1 Estimate the perimeter of the rectangle.

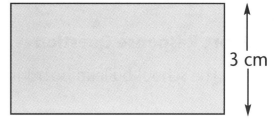

3 cm

   A 6 cm   **C** 18 cm

   B 12 cm   **D** 3 cm

2 What measurement tool would you use to find the perimeter of the rectangle in Problem 1?

   F metric ruler   **H** metric scale

   G Celsius thermometer   **J** none of the above

3 Kim's mother wants to measure a window for blinds. What measurement tool should she use to find the area in centimeters?

A meter stick   **C** metric ruler

B yardstick   **D** Celsius thermometer

4 Derek wants to measure the square shown below with a meter stick. Carlos wants to use a metric ruler. Which is the more appropriate tool? _____ Why?

_____

_____

5 What measurement tool would you use to measure the following items?

length of a car _____   perimeter of a rug _____

area of a trampoline _____   cold lemonade _____

50-yd dash _____   pot of soup _____

Short Response Question

6 The school bulletin board measures 2 meters by 3 meters.

Part A What is the area of the bulletin board? _____ Show your work.

Part B The class is working on an art project using paper about the size of notebook paper. What metric measurement tool should be used to measure the area of each sheet of paper in order to find out how many pieces of paper will fit on the bulletin board? Explain your answer.

_____

_____

Lesson 5.10 ▪ Compare equivalent measures within the metric system

 Think About It

Sometimes you need to change the unit of measure. The line below is one decimeter long. How many centimeters will it measure?

_____

 Here's How

Use a metric ruler.

The line measures _____ cm.

Use an equivalency chart.

Metric Units of Measurement
      1 kilometer = 1,000 meters
          1 meter = 100 centimeters
          1 meter = 10 decimeters
      1 decimeter = 10 centimeters
      1 centimeter = 10 millimeters

In this case, the answer is given in the equivalency chart: 1 dm = _____ cm

How many centimeters will a line measure if it is 3 dm long?

_____ × 10 cm = _____ cm

 Practice

Fill in the blanks with the equivalent measure. Show your work.

1 40 cm = ____ dm

2 ____ cm = 5 m

3 500 m = ____ km

4 5 dm = ____ cm

5 ____ km = 2,000 m

6 9 cm = ____ mm

7 Kim's mother measures a window for blinds using her hand. The width of her hand is about 1 decimeter. She finds that the window is about 6 dm wide and 10 dm high. Estimate what the window measures in centimeters.

   A 600 cm × 100 cm

   C 60 cm × 1 cm

   B 60 cm × 100 cm

   D 12 cm × 20 cm

8 Use the measurements of the window in Problem 7 to estimate the following:

perimeter of the window _____ dm

perimeter of the window _____ cm

area of the window _____ sq dm

area of the window _____ sq cm

9 The perimeter of Bill's backyard measures 500 meters. The perimeter of Betty's backyard measures 40,000 decimeters. Whose backyard has the largest perimeter? Show your work.

_____

10 John walked 4 kilometers for his favorite charity. How many meters did he walk? Show your work.

_____ m

Short Response Question

11 If a race is 1 kilometer long, how many 50-meter laps must be run to finish the race? Show your work and explain your answer.

_____

_____

_____

Lesson 5.11 ▪ Perimeter of polygons

> **READY REFERENCE**
> **polygon** closed plane figure with sides made up of connected line segments
> **perimeter** the distance around the sides of a polygon

 Think About It

How do you find the perimeter of this polygon?

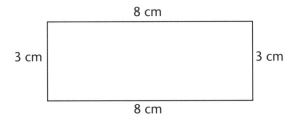

8 cm

3 cm   3 cm

8 cm

 Here's How

Find the perimeter by using addition.

The perimeter can be found by adding the length of each side.

_____ cm + _____ cm + _____ cm + _____ cm = _____ cm

Find the perimeter by using multiplication.

You can use multiplication to find the perimeter of a rectangle. In this rectangle, two of the sides measure 8 cm and two of the sides measure 3 cm.

8 cm × 2 = _____ cm   3 cm × 2 = _____ cm

The perimeter of the rectangle is _____ cm + _____ cm = _____ cm

The perimeter can be found by using the following formula.

Perimeter = (length × 2) + (width × 2)

= (_____ × 2) + (_____ × 2)

= _____ + _____

= _____

🔑 Practice

Find the perimeter of the polygon in each problem.

1

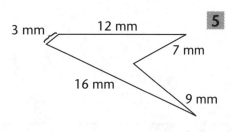

6 in

3 in   3 in

6 in

perimeter = _____

2

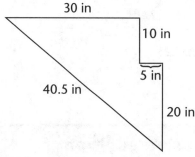

10 yd

10.5 yd   14 yd

20 yd

perimeter = _____

3

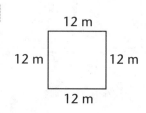

10 ft   10 ft

10 ft   10 ft

10 ft   10 ft

perimeter = _____

4

3 mm   12 mm

7 mm

16 mm

9 mm

perimeter = _____

5

30 in

10 in

5 in

40.5 in

20 in

perimeter = _____

6

12 m

12 m   12 m

12 m

perimeter = _____

7 Rob's room is a square with each side measuring 11 ft. What is the perimeter of his room? Use a formula to find the perimeter. Show your work.

_____

8 Find the perimeter of a triangle with sides that each measure 25 cm. Find the perimeter three different ways. Show your work.

Short Response Question

9   Kenesha's yard needs to be fenced for her new puppy. What is the perimeter of her yard? _____ Show your work.

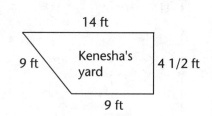

14 ft

9 ft   Kenesha's yard   4 1/2 ft

9 ft

Can you use the perimeter formula to solve this problem? _____ Explain your answer.

_____

_____

Lesson 5.12 ▪ Find the circumference of circles

READY REFERENCE

circumference distance around a circle

diameter a line segment that passes through the center of a circle and has both endpoints on the circle

endpoint point at the end of a line segment

radius a line segment with one endpoint at the center of a circle and the other on the circle

Think About It

What is the circumference of the circle to the right?
What is the diameter of the circle?
What is the radius of the circle?

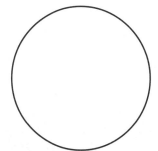

Here's How

Step 1 Place a piece of string around the circle and cut the string.

Step 2 Measure the piece of string with a ruler. This is the circumference of the circle. The circumference of the circle is _____ inches.

Step 3 Cut a piece of string equal to the length of the diameter of the circle.

Step 4 Compare the piece of string to the piece of string that equals the circumference of the circle. Are they the same length? _____ How many pieces of string the length of the diameter equal the length of the string for the circumference of the circle? _____ Diameter = _____ in

Step 5 Divide the length of the diameter by 2 to find the radius.
Radius = _____ in

Practice

Use a piece of string to measure the circumference of each circle in problems 1–4.

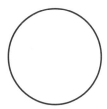

circumference = _____

circumference = _____

3

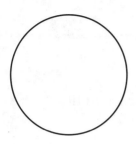

circumference = _____

4

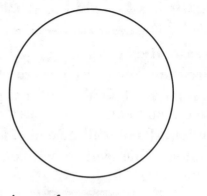

circumference = _____

Use the measurements to calculate the following.

5

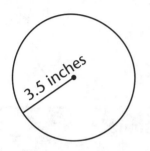

3.5 inches

diameter = _____

6

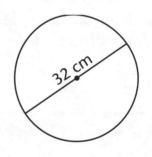

32 cm

radius = _____

Short Response Question

7 Adrian wants to make a rock garden in the shape of a circle. The landscaper asks him what the circumference of the garden will be.

Part A How should Adrian measure the space he intends to use for the garden?

_____

_____

Part B If the circumference of the rock garden is 4 yards, what are the radius and the diameter of the garden? Show your work.

radius _____

diameter _____

Lesson 5.13 ▪ Graphing data

 Think About It

The manager of Snyder's Grocery Store is thinking of hiring a cashier for 3 hours on Saturdays. She made this graph. It shows store traffic during an 8-hour period last Saturday. Analyze the graph to find which 3-hour period the cashier should work.

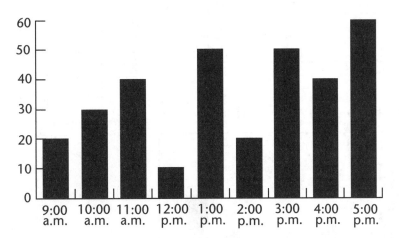

Here's How

Step 1 Find out what each axis of the graph shows.

1. What does the vertical axis show? _____

2. What does the horizontal axis show? _____

Step 2 Find out what number each bar shows.

3. Write the number of people in the store for each time.

9:00 _____ 10:00 _____ 11:00 _____ 12:00 _____ 1:00 _____

2:00 _____ 3:00 _____ 4:00 _____ 5:00 _____

Step 3 Find the information to answer the question.

4. Which group of three bars in a row is the tallest?

_____

5. For what 3-hour period should a new person be hired?

_____

Practice

1 Emilio's school newspaper contains a chart showing the distance some of the students live from the school. Shade in the bar graph to reflect the data found in the chart.

Miles	Students
1/4	ꟷꟷꟷꟷꟷ ꟷꟷꟷꟷꟷ
1/2	ꟷꟷꟷꟷꟷ |||
1	ꟷꟷꟷꟷꟷ ꟷꟷꟷꟷꟷ ꟷꟷꟷꟷꟷ
More than 1	ꟷꟷꟷꟷꟷ ꟷꟷꟷꟷꟷ ꟷꟷꟷꟷꟷ |||

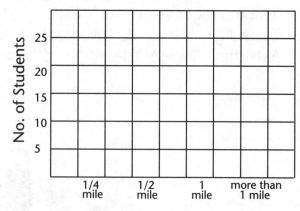

Use the graph below to answer Problems 2 – 4.

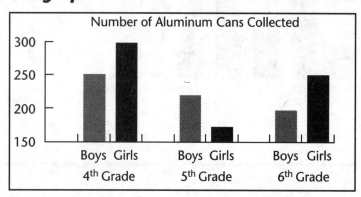

2 What does this graph show? _____

3 Which grade collected the most cans? _____

4 Which group of girls collected the most cans? _____

5 Which group of boys collected about 250 cans? _____

Extended Response Question

6 Make a bar graph using the following high and low temperatures: New York City–high 72°, low 57°; Albany–high 71°, low 54°; Buffalo–high 78°, low 52°; Rochester–high 76°, low 52°. How do bar graphs help you understand data?

Lesson 5.14 ▪ Make frequency tables from tallied data

> **READY REFERENCE**
> **frequency** the number of times a number occurs in a set

 Think About It

Mrs. Clymer asked 30 students how many hours of television they watched during one week. She wrote the collected data on the chalkboard. Make a frequency table from the data.

0-5 hours	JHT I
6-10 hours	IIII
11-15 hours	JHT JHT
16-20 hours	JHT III
21-25 hours	II

 Here's How

Step 1 Write a title for the table telling what the table is about.

_____

Step 2 Determine how many cells, or boxes, of information are needed for the table and draw the table in the space below.

Step 3 Label each cell telling what information will be in the column.

Step 4 Fill in the frequency table with the tallied data.

🔑 Practice

Use the frequency table in Here's How to answer the following questions.

1 How many hours of television did the greatest number of students watch each week?

    A 24 hours   **B** 6 hours   **C** 18 hours   **D** 30 hours

2 How many students watch more than 20 hours of television each week?

    F 2   **G** 6   **H** 18   **J** 10

Use the frequency table below to answer Problems 4 and 5.

MONEY EARNED AT HOME EACH WEEK BY THE STUDENTS IN MR. POE'S CLASS	
Amount earned	**Number of students**
$ 2.00	4
$ 5.00	12
$10.00	3

3 How many students earned $10.00 per week? _____

4 What was the amount earned most frequently by the students? _____

Short Response Question
Make a frequency table from the data below.

5 The high temperature for each day in the month of January was recorded in a tally chart. Ten days had temperatures 15°–20° F, 6 days had temperatures 20°–25° F, 3 days had temperatures 25°–30° F, and 12 days had temperatures 30°–35° F.

Lesson 5.15 ▪ Organize data with graphs, models, pictures, and lists

 Think About It

Mr. Fontaine's fourth-grade class gathered data on basketball. First they surveyed 4 students in the class to find out how many games of basketball each student had played during the past month. Mario had played 15 games, Nora had played 20 games, Phillip had played 5 games, and Sam had played 10 games. How can the class organize this data?

 Here's How

Make a list.

List the students' names and the number of games each student played.

Students–Games played

_____ – 20

Mario – 15

Sam – _____

_____ – ____

Make a pictograph.

Number of Games Played	
Mario	🏀 🏀 🏀
Nora	🏀 🏀 🏀 🏀
Phillip	🏀
Sam	🏀 🏀
Each 🏀 stands for __ games.	

Make a circle graph or a bar graph.

Fill in the missing information in the circle graph. Shade in the number of games in the bar graph.

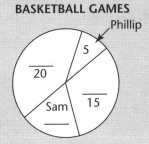

BASKETBALL GAMES

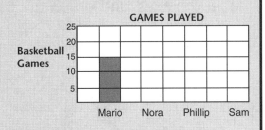

GAMES PLAYED

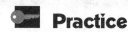 **Practice**

1 Mr. Chung's class read 65 books in 1999, 70 books in 1996, 60 books in 1997, and 50 books in 1998. Make a list organizing the data from greatest to least.

_____

Now, list the data by year, from the earliest to the latest.

_____

Use the pictograph to answer Problems 2–3.

2 In which year were the most books read? _____

3 How many books did the 1996 class read? _____

Number of Books Read	
1999	🕮🕮🕮🕮🕮🕮🕮
1998	🕮🕮🕮🕮🕮
1997	🕮🕮🕮🕮🕮🕮
1996	🕮🕮🕮🕮🕮🕮🕮

Each 🕮 stands for 10 books.

Use the line graph to answer Problems 4–5.

4 Did the number of books read decrease or increase between 1996 and 1997? _____

5 Was the number of books read in 1999 greater or less than in 1996?

_____

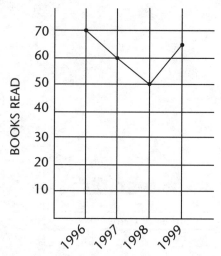

Short Response Question

6 Cameron's class surveyed students to find out what kind of pets they had. They found the following data: 30 dogs, 45 cats, 40 fish, and 15 birds. Make a bar graph showing the number of students who own each type of pet. Give your graph a title, label the axes, and graph the data. Write a statement comparing pet ownership.

_____

_____

Lesson 5.16 ▪ Average or arithmetic mean

> **READY REFERENCE**
> **mean** the sum of the addends divided by the number of addends; the average

🔑 Think About It

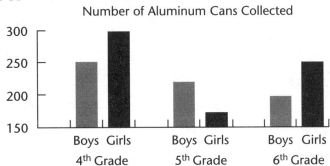

Number of Aluminum Cans Collected

What is the mean or average number of cans collected by the boys?

🔑 Here's How

Step 1 Add the number of cans collected by the boys in each grade.

Collected by boys: 250 + 225 + 200 = _____

Step 2 Divide the sum by the number of addends (number of grade levels).

_____ ÷ 3 = _____

Answer: _____ is the mean number of cans collected by the boys.

🔑 Practice

Use the bar graph in Think About It **to answer Problems 1–2.**

1 What is the mean number of cans collected by the girls? Show your work.

A 300   **B** 725   **C** $241\frac{2}{3}$ **D** 3

2 What is the mean number of cans collected by grade 4? Show your work.

F 550   **G** 6   **H** 3   **J** 275

3 What is the mean number of hours spent watching television during one week by the students in Mrs. Clymer's class? _____ Show your work.

Hours	Number of Students
7	6
10	4
19	10
20	8
24	2

Find the mean for each set of data. Show your work.

4 7, 2, 9, 8, 4   **5** 30, 19, 30, 21   **6** 46, 19, 40

_____   _____   _____

◆ Short Response Question

7 Use counters for this problem.

Apples picked on Saturday	
Angela	🍎🍎🍎
Barry	🍎🍎🍎🍎
Juan	🍎🍎
Each 🍎 stands for 20 apples	

Part A Use 9 counters. Each counter represents one of the symbols on the pictograph or 20 apples. Divide the counters into three equal groups. How many counters are in each group? _____

Part B Find the mean for the apples picked on Saturday. _____ Show your work.

Part C Is your answer the same number as in Part A? ____ Explain your answer.

_____

_____

Lesson 5.17 ▪ Find the range and the mean

> **READY REFERENCE**
> **range** in a set of data, the difference between the greatest number and the least number

Think About It

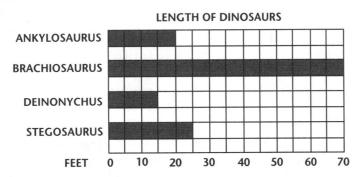

LENGTH OF DINOSAURS

What is the range and mean in the length of the dinosaurs?

Here's How

Find the range.

Step 1 What is the length of the longest dinosaur? _____

Step 2 What is the length of the shortest dinosaur? _____

Step 3 Find the difference between the greatest number and the least number. The difference is the range.

$$\begin{array}{r} 70 \quad \longleftarrow \text{ greatest number} \\ -15 \quad \longleftarrow \text{ least number} \\ \hline \underline{\quad} \quad \longleftarrow \text{ range} \end{array}$$

Find the mean.

Step 1 Add the lengths of the dinosaurs. _____ + _____ + _____ + 25 = _____

Step 2 Divide the sum by the number of dinosaurs (the number of addends). _____ ÷ 4 = _____ The quotient is the mean or the average length of the dinosaurs.

Practice

Find the range and the mean in each problem. Show your work.

1

Day	High Temperature
Monday	37°
Tuesday	43°
Wednesday	41°
Thursday	30°
Friday	34°

range: _____

mean: _____

2

Day	Low Temperature
Monday	28°
Tuesday	36°
Wednesday	35°
Thursday	26°
Friday	30°

range: _____

mean: _____

3

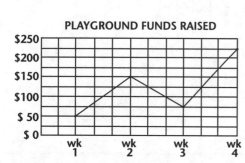

range: _____

mean: _____

4

Science Fair Attendance

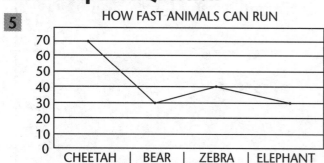

range: _____

mean: _____

Short Response Question

5

HOW FAST ANIMALS CAN RUN

CHEETAH	BEAR	ZEBRA	ELEPHANT

Part A What is the range in speeds of the animals? _____ Show your work.

Part B What is the mean? _____ Show your work.

Directions

Use a separate piece of paper to show your work.

1 A paper clip is about 1 centimeter wide. Estimate whether each item will measure more or less than 1 cm.

notebook paper _____

apple _____

pencil point _____

2 Write the letter of the appropriate measurement tool.

your tennis shoe _____

a roasting chicken _____

a library table _____

today's recess time _____

A metric ruler   **C** clock

B meterstick   **D** metric scale

3 Donna and Juanita are going shopping at the mall. How much time do they plan to spend at the mall?

Arrive at the Mall   **Leave the Mall**

F 2 hr 50 min
G 1 hr 5 min
H 3 hr 15 min
J 2 hr 10 min

4 Jan's cousin asked her to design place cards for a dinner party. Jan selected a place card 7 cm by 3 cm. What is the perimeter of the card?

Answer _____

What would the perimeter be if the length and width were each increased by 3 cm?

Answer _____

5 Make a line graph using the information in the table.

Day	Test Score
Monday	85
Wednesday	80
Friday	90

6 Look at the scores in Problem 5. Find the mean test score.

Answer _____

Lesson 6.1 ▪ Rounding numbers

> **READY REFERENCE**
>
> **round** write a number as the nearest ten, hundred, or thousand

🔑 Think About It

T-shirts need to be ordered for the school field trip. On Monday, 23 students have signed up to go on the trip. About how many T-shirts will be needed, rounded to the nearest ten?

🔑 Here's How

Use a number line.

1. How do you round 23 to the nearest ten? The number 23 is between 20 and 30. It is less than halfway between 20 and 30, so 23 is rounded to 20. About _____ T-shirts will be needed. Rule: When a number is less than halfway, round down.

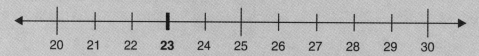

2. By Friday, 28 students have signed up. The T-shirts have not been ordered yet. About how many are needed now? (Round your answer to the nearest ten) The number 28 is between 20 and 30. It is more than halfway, so about _____ T-shirts are needed. Rule: When a number is more than halfway, round _____.

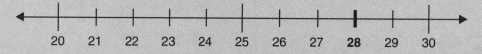

3. Rule: When a number is exactly halfway, round up.

Use measuring instruments.

Measuring instruments such as a yardstick or a thermometer can also be used to help you in rounding numbers.

1. The temperature Monday was 88 degrees. Rounded to the nearest ten, it was about 90 degrees. Tuesday's temperature was only 82 degrees. Rounded to the nearest ten, it was about _____ degrees.

🔑 Practice

Round to the nearest ten.

1 49 _____   **2** 46 _____   **3** 42 _____   **4** 45 _____   **5** 41 _____

Round to the nearest hundred.

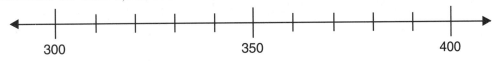

6 335 _____   **7** 380 _____   **8** 349 _____   **9** 310 _____

Round to the nearest thousand.

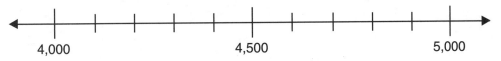

10 4,160 _____   **11** 4,399 _____   **12** 4,588 _____   **13** 4,789 _____

🏠 Short Response Question

14 Use each thermometer to find the temperature and round it to the nearest ten. Explain the rule you used to round the temperature.

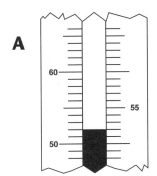

A   temperature: _____   rounded temperature: _____

_____

_____

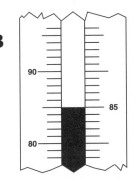

B   temperature: _____   rounded temperature: _____

_____

_____

Lesson 6.2 ▪ Estimate measurements

> **READY REFERENCE**
>
> **comparisons** examinations of objects to see how they are alike so that a measurement can be estimated

🔑 Think About It

Which is larger—a golf ball or a baseball? Why do you think a baseball would weigh more than a golf ball? Name some balls that would probably weigh more than a baseball.

🔑 Here's How

People use their own ways of estimating measurements every day. Look at the pictures below. Then answer the questions that follow.

1. Which object is the largest? _____

2. Which object is the smallest? _____

3. Which object will probably weigh the most? _____

   The least? _____

4. Which objects will probably have almost the same weight? _____

   How do you know? _____

🔑 Practice

1 There are about five sheets of paper in one ounce. How many ounces would a report weigh if it was 20 pages long?

_____

2 A size 10 shoe is about ten inches long. A person who wears this size shoe can cross a parking lot in 120 heel-to-toe steps. How many inches across is the parking lot?

_____

3 Carol's basketball goal is nine feet off the ground. She is five feet three inches tall. Follow the steps below to figure out how much taller the goal is than Carol.

How many inches shorter than six feet is Carol? _____ What is the difference in height from six feet to nine feet? _____ How many feet and inches taller is the basketball goal than Carol? _____

4 There are 1,000 milliliters in one liter. You need 3,500 milliliters of water to fill a fish bowl. All you have is a one-liter bottle. How many bottles of water will probably fill this fish bowl?

_____

Short Response Question

5 Look at the picture on the bulletin board. The bulletin board is 1 meter wide. Estimate the width of the picture in centimeters. Explain how you arrived at your estimate.

| ⊢———— **1 meter** ————⊣ | **Estimate** _____ cm |

_____

_____

_____

_____

Lesson 6.3 ▪ Compare estimates with results

🔑 Think About It

Rounded numbers can be used when estimating the answer to a problem. You can use the estimate to check your answer when you complete the problem.

🔑 Here's How

Use rounding.

Step 1 Round each number to the nearest thousand. Add.

$$3,589 \longrightarrow 4,000$$
$$+ 2,789 \longrightarrow + 3,000$$

Write your estimate ⟶ _____

Step 2 Solve the problem.

$$3,589$$
$$+ 2,789$$

Write the answer ⟶ _____

Step 3 Compare the answer to your estimate. Is your answer reasonable?

Use front-end estimation.

Step 1 Add the numbers in the thousands place for a lower limit.

$$\begin{array}{r} \mathbf{3,589} \\ + \mathbf{2,789} \\ \hline \mathbf{5} \end{array}$$ ⟵ Low estimate of 5,000

Step 2 Raise all the numbers to the next thousands place for an upper limit.

$$4,000 + 3,000 = \underline{\hspace{2cm}}$$ ⟵ High estimate

Step 3 The sum should be greater than 5,000 and less than _____.

🔑 Practice

Estimate by rounding the numbers to the highest place value and writing the problem. Then solve the problem and compare your answers.

1
$$\begin{array}{r} 541 \\ + 367 \\ \hline \end{array}$$

2
$$\begin{array}{r} 680 \\ - 268 \\ \hline \end{array}$$

3
$$\begin{array}{r} 1,349 \\ + 3,681 \\ \hline \end{array}$$

4 8,640
     − 3,300

5 $8.78
     + 3.25

6 $55.89
     − 12.35

Use front-end estimation to find a high and low estimate. Solve the problem. Compare the result with your estimate.

7   567   high estimate _____
     + 432   low estimate _____

8   9,768   high estimate _____
     + 2,324   low estimate _____

9   2,608   high estimate _____
     ×   2   low estimate _____

10 $4,255   high estimate _____
        9,128   low estimate _____
      + 6,509

Short Response Question

Use front-end estimation to find a high and a low estimate, and then solve the problem. Compare your estimate to the answer. Show your work and explain why your estimate is reasonable.

11 There were 3,429 fans for the home team and 2,945 fans for the visitors. How many fans were in the stadium?

_____

_____

_____

Lesson 6.4 ▪ Explore the meaning of large numbers

🔑 Think About It

Do you think understanding large numbers such as millions is important? There are some things that can only be described using large numbers. Certain sales figures are in the millions of dollars. Millions of pairs of socks are sold each year.

🔑 Here's How

Nicole's new hobby is making bead necklaces. Her favorite beads come in packets of 100, but it is cheaper to buy the packets by the box. Each box contains 10 packets. How many beads are there in each box? _____

Nicole started a chart to calculate the number of beads. Complete Nicole's chart.

Boxes of Beads	Number of Beads
1 Box	1,000
10 Boxes	10,000
100 Boxes	
1,000 Boxes	

1. How many boxes would Nicole buy to get 1,000,000 beads?

_____

2. How many 1,000s are in 1,000,000? _____

🔑 Practice

Use a library or reading book. Show your work.

1 Estimate the number of alphabet letters on one page. _____

2 Estimate the number of pages containing 1,000 alphabet letters. _____

3 Estimate the number of pages containing 100,000 letters. _____

4 10 × 1 = _____

5 10 × 10 = _____

6 10 × 100 = _____

7 10 × 1,000 = _____

8 10 × 10,000 = _____

9 10 × 100,000 = _____

10 How many 100s equal 1,000? _____

How many 1,000s equal 10,000? _____

How many 10,000s equal 100,000? _____

How many 100,000s equal 1,000,000? _____

Short Response Question

11 Allison knows that a coffee can will hold one pound of rice. There are about 20,000 grains of rice in one pound. How many coffee cans would it take to hold one million grains of rice? Show your work and explain your answer.

_____

_____

_____

Lesson 6.5 ▪ Real-world examples of when estimating is acceptable

> **READY REFERENCE**
> **estimate** to give an approximate answer rather than an exact answer

🔑 Think About It

When is it okay to round or to estimate in real-life situations? It depends on how exact the answer has to be. If you need to know about how many or need to decide if there are enough, you can probably estimate.

🔑 Here's How

Part 1 Megan's favorite cookie recipe calls for $1\frac{3}{4}$ cups of sugar, $2\frac{1}{3}$ cups of flour, and $\frac{3}{4}$ cups of shortening. She is in a hurry, and it would save time for her to round the ingredients to the nearest cup. Round the ingredients to the nearest whole cup.

_____ cups sugar   _____ cups flour   _____ cup shortening

_____   _____   _____

Will her cookies have a good chance of winning a blue ribbon at the state fair? Do you think they will taste right? Think about whether there will be too much or not enough of any of the ingredients. Write *too much* or *not enough* under each rounded measurement above.

Part 2 Alf's cousin is coming to visit next week. His family is driving and expects the trip to take $3\frac{3}{4}$ hours. Alf estimates it will take about _____ hours. Do you think it is okay to estimate in this situation? _____ Why or why not?

_____

_____

_____

🔑 Practice

Read the following problem and circle **estimate** *or* **exact.** *Explain your answers.*

1 The local ballpark held a softball tournament to raise money to build a new playing field. The cost of the new field is $600. Sixteen teams each paid $25.00 to play. Sixteen moms and 18 dads signed up to help run the tournament. Ninety-two spectators paid $3.00 each to watch the games.

Part A How much did the teams pay in total to play in the tournament? Would you estimate or find an exact answer?
Estimate   Exact   Explain. _____

Part B There are 40 hats available for the volunteer moms and dads to wear. Are there enough hats?
Estimate   Exact   Explain. _____

Part C How much money was raised from ticket sales to spectators?
Estimate   Exact   Explain. _____

Part D Did the tournament bring in enough money to pay for the new playing field?
Estimate   Exact   Explain. _____

2 Kathryn's last basketball game is scheduled for 7 p.m. tonight. Her mother estimates it will take about 15 minutes to stop at the store for snacks and 18 minutes to drive from the store to the game. About what time should she arrive at the store to make it to the game on time?

_____

_____

Short Response Question

3 Write a problem in which an estimate would be acceptable as an answer. Then write a problem in which an estimate would NOT be acceptable as an answer. Explain your thinking.

_____

_____

_____

Lesson 6.6 ▪ The meaning of *million*

🔑 Think About It

When you hear the word "million" what comes to your mind?

🔑 Here's How

Imagine that you have one million dollars. The money can only be spent on movies. You can attend one movie a day every day of the year. The movie tickets are $5.00 each. How long would it take you to spend the million dollars?

1. How many movies can you see? _____

   n = the number of movies

   $$\frac{\$1,000,000}{\$5} = n$$

   $n = 200,000$

2. How many years it will take you to spend your million dollars?

   200,000 movies ÷ 365 days = _____

   Round 365 to the nearest hundred = _____

   $400\overline{)200,000}$ = _____ years

3. It would take me _____ years to spend $1,000,000 on movies if I could see _____ movie a day and each movie cost $_____.

🔑 Practice

1	2	3
100,000 × 10	10,000 × 100	1,000 × 1,000

4 Ramon's father has a delivery business. He needs 100 new trucks. The local dealership is going to sell him new trucks for $10,000 each. How much will it cost Ramon's father to buy the trucks?

_____

5 Stacy's favorite video game has a perfect score of 100,000 points. How many times will she have to play the game to score 1,000,000 points? _____

6 There are 985 children each writing a 1,000-word mystery story. Estimate the total number of words the children will write. _____

7 About 800,000 New Yorkers work in banking.
How close is 800,000 to one million?   _____

Is 800,000 closer to one million or half a million? _____

How do you know? _____

_____

Short Response Question

Show your work and explain your answers.

8 Beth lives in New York City. New York City has a population of 7,322,564, or about seven million people. Albany's population is 101,082. Albany is 138 miles from New York City. Estimate how many trips to Albany it would take Beth to travel one million miles.

_____

About how many cities with populations the size of Albany's would it take to have the same number of people as in New York City?

_____

_____

_____

_____

Lesson 6.7 ▪ Rounding numbers

> **READY REFERENCE**
>
> **rounding** writing a number to the nearest tenth, whole number, ten, hundred, or thousand

 Think About It

Knowing how to round numbers is helpful when you are asked to estimate an amount. When discussing age, we often round to the nearest ten. For example: Sandy is about 20 years old. Josiah is about 80 years old.

Sometimes it is important to round miles to the nearest tenth. Example: Turn right and go 5.3 miles to our driveway.

 Here's How

Sandy is 23 years old. Josiah is 76 years old. Round their ages to the nearest ten.

Step 1 Find the digit in the place to be rounded. Underline that number.

2<u>3</u>   1<u>6</u>

Step 2 Look at the digit to the right of the number you underlined. If it is 5 or more, round up. If it is less than 5, round to the number already underlined.

2<u>3</u>   3 is less than 5, so 23 rounds to 20.

8<u>6</u>   6 is more than 5, so 86 rounds to _____ .

Molly was invited to a birthday party. Her friend lives 2.48 miles from her house. Round the distance to the nearest tenth of a mile.

Step 1 2.<u>4</u>8

Step 2 2.<u>4</u>8   _____ is more than _____ , so 2.48 rounds to _____ .

 Practice

Round to the nearest tenth.

1 35.679 _____   **2** 4.539 _____   **3** 62.261 _____

4 2.39 _____   **5** 147.889 _____   **6** 0.39 _____

Round to the nearest whole number.

7 35.679 _____   **8** 4.539 _____   **9** 8.91 _____

Round to the nearest hundred.

10 868 _____   **11** 1,531 _____   **12** 210.9 _____

Round to the nearest thousand.

13 5,901 _____   **14** 1,498 _____   **15** 9,511.9 _____

Read each problem. Estimate by rounding.

16 The odometer on Ken's family's car reads 23,541 miles. About how many thousands of miles has the car been driven? _____

17 Mariana's supplies for art camp cost $18.95. About how much money will she need for the supplies? _____

Short Response Question

18 Robert has three books to read. The first book has 157 pages, the second book has 221 pages, and the third book has 258 pages. About how many pages will he have read after he finishes all three books? Show your work and explain your answer.

_____

_____

Lesson 6.8 ▪ More estimation strategies

> **READY REFERENCE**
>
> **clustering** estimating by rounding all the numbers to the same number and then multiplying
>
> **compatible numbers** numbers that are easily computed mentally; two numbers, one of which divides the other evenly
>
> **estimate** an approximate answer
>
> **front-end estimation** finding an approximate answer by using the digits in the place with the greatest value

 Think About It

You know how to round numbers. There are other strategies that you can use to find estimates when adding, subtracting, multiplying, and dividing.

Here's How

Use front-end estimation to estimate sums, differences, or products.	**126 × 4**
Step 1 Multiply front-end digits.	100 × 4 = _____
Step 2 To make your estimate more accurate, round the remaining numbers. Round 26 to 30.	30 × 4 = _____
Step 3 Add the products.	400 + 120 = _____
Use compatible numbers to estimate a quotient.	**357 ÷ 5**
Use numbers that are easy to compute mentally and are close to the original numbers.	350 ÷ 5 = _____
Use clustering to estimate a sum.	**433 + 392 + 401 + 397**
All of the addends cluster around 400.	400 + 400 + 400 + 400 = _____
	4 × 400 = _____

 **Practice**

Rewrite each problem with rounded numbers, and solve.

1
```
  2,351
+ 6,559
```

2
```
  566
− 414
```

3
```
  879
× 22
```

4 398 ÷ 18

Use front-end estimation. Round the remaining numbers, and solve.

5
```
  521
+ 232
```

6
```
  267
×   2
```

7
```
  680
− 214
```

Estimate each quotient by using compatible numbers.

8 85 ÷ 6

9 192 ÷ 53

10 286 ÷ 33

Short Response Question

11 Enrique's family drove to the mountains for their vacation. They drove 489 miles on the first day, 512 miles on the second day, 498 miles on the third day, and 509 days on the fourth day. About how many miles did Enrique's family drive? Show your work and explain the strategy you used.

_____

_____

_____

Lesson 6.9 ▪ Estimating quantities

> **READY REFERENCE**
>
> **mental math** solving a problem in your head
>
> **compensation** a mental math tool in which a sum, difference, product, or quotient is made easier by using easier numbers, such as tens or hundreds

Think About It

Marcus has saved $14.90 each week for 2 weeks. About how much money has he saved? How can you calculate the answer using mental math?

Here's How

Estimate by rounding.	$14.90 × 2 = $14.90 + $14.90
Step 1 Round $14.90 to the nearest dollar.	$ _____
Step 2 Add the rounded numbers.	$15 + $15 = $ _____
So, Marcus has about $ _____ after saving for 2 weeks.	
Estimate by using compensation.	**$14.90 + $14.90**
Step 1 Add 10¢ to $14.90 to make $15.00. $15.00 is easier to use than $14.90.	$15 + $15 = _____
Step 2 Subtract 20¢ from the sum to compensate for adding 20¢ extra.	$30.00 − .20 = $ _____
$14.90 + $14.90 = _____	

Practice

Estimate by rounding to the nearest dollar.

1 $52.99
      × _____ 5

2 $129.76
      + 234.13

3 $4,073.89
      − 3,544.10

4 $26.77
      − 15.82
      ⎯⎯⎯⎯⎯

5 $359.85
      ×   4
      ⎯⎯⎯⎯⎯

6 $8,999.99
        4,554.87
      + 1,280.15
      ⎯⎯⎯⎯⎯

Estimate by using compensation. Show your work.

7 1,989 + 11 =

8 $45.13 × 5 =

9 6,500 − 3,995 =

10 Sarah's favorite paperback books cost $6.85 each. About how much money will she have to save to buy the entire set of 12?

11 The movie theater seats 98 people. Tickets cost $5.85 each. About how much money will the theater earn if every seat is sold?

Short Response Question

12 Ramon's older brother has a part-time job. He earns $85.75 a week. Ramon earns $12.25 a week. If they each save all their money for a year, about how much money will they have? Show your work and explain your answer.

_____

_____

_____

Lesson 6.10 • Strategies for estimating measurements

 Think About It

Can you estimate the length, width, weight, and capacity of objects? About how long is your pencil? About how many pounds does that rock weigh? About how many ounces of water do you have?

 Here's How

Length

Look at the point of the pencil. What mark on the ruler is it closest to? It is closest to the _____ inch mark. The pencil is about _____ inches long.

Weight

Locate the arrow on the scale. What pound mark is it closest to? It is closest to the _____ pound mark. The rock weighs about _____ pounds.

Capacity

Where is the level of the water? It is halfway between _____ and _____ ounces. There are about _____ ounces of water.

 **Practice**

1 Which pen is about 4 inches long?

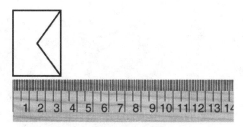

A
Inches

C
Inches

B
Inches

D
Inches

2 About how wide is the envelope?

A 4 centimeters   **B** 3 centimeters   **C** 8 centimeters   **D** none of the answers

3 About how much do the oranges weigh?

A 2 pounds   **C** $2\frac{1}{2}$ pounds

B 3 pounds   **D** None of the above

Short Response Question

4 Which 2 glasses of water would add up to about 9 ounces of water?
Explain your answer.

Figure 1   **Figure 2**   **Figure 3**

_____

_____

Lesson 6.11 ▪ Determining arrangements and combinations

 Think About It

When you play a game, you try to think of everything that might happen. These are called possible outcomes. They are also called combinations. Knowing possible outcomes can help you plan your next move.

 Here's How

Matthew has a new game with two spinners. He must spin both spinners on each turn. How many possible outcomes are there?

Spinner 1 **Spinner 2**

Step 1 List the possible outcomes for Spinner 1.

black

white

_____ **possible outcomes: black or white**

Step 2 Add the possible outcomes for Spinner 2 to each possible outcome for Spinner 1.

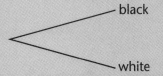

black
1
2
3

white
1
2
3

_____ **possible outcomes for black and 3 for white**

Step 3 Add up all the possible outcomes.

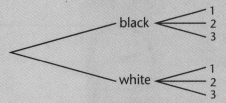

black
1 — B1
2 — B2
3 — B3

white
1 — W1
2 — W2
3 — W3

_____ **possible outcomes in all**

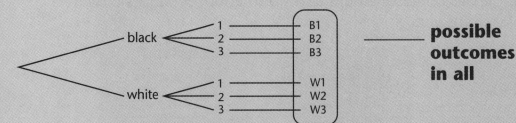

This picture of the possible outcomes is called a tree diagram. Notice that the answer 6 is the product of the possible outcomes for each act or step: $2 \times 3 = 6$. This is called the **counting principle.**

Practice

1 You flip a coin, roll a number cube, and spin a spinner with 4 numbers. Using the counting principle, how many possible outcomes are there?

A 2×6 **B** $2 \times 2 \times 4$ **C** $2 \times 6 \times 4$ **D** $4 \times 6 \times 4$

2 How many different ways can you arrange four paintings on a wall in a row from left to right?

F 6 **G** 12 **H** 24 **J** 48

3 You have three coins—a dime, a nickel, and a quarter. How many ways can you stack the coins with the nickel on top?

A 1 **B** 2 **C** 3 **D** 6

4 Make a tree diagram to show the possible combinations. How many combinations are possible if you choose one main dish and one vegetable dish?

Today's Menu:	Main Dishes:
	Turkey Breast • Ham Steak • Chicken Pot Pie
	Vegetables:
	Baked Potato • Corn on the Cob • Lima Beans

Short Response Question

5 There are three jobs at the hot dog stand. One job is cooking **(C)**, one is serving hot dogs **(M)**, and one is running the register **(R)**. Your co-workers are Suki and Keith. Each person can do one job at a time. Make a list of the possible combinations for filling the jobs. How many combinations are there? Show your work.

Lesson 6.12 ▪ Estimation and calculators

> **READY REFERENCE**
> **decimal**   a number with one or more places to the right of the decimal point; *example:* 0.4, 6.02

 Think About It

Sometimes it is useful to first estimate the result of a computation and then use a calculator to check the estimate. Comparing the estimate and the answer you get using a calculator will tell you if the estimate was reasonable.

Marie's bicycle club wants to find out about how many miles they have traveled so far this week. Monday they traveled 6.5 miles, Tuesday they traveled 3.8 miles, and Wednesday they bicycled almost all day and traveled 20.39 miles. About how many miles did they travel?

 Here's How

Estimate by rounding.

1. Look at the digit in the tenths place.

2. 6.**5** 5 rounds up, so 6.5 rounds to _____.

3. 3.**8** 8 rounds up because 8 _____ 5. So 3.8 rounds to _____.

4. 20.**3**9 3 rounds down because 3 _____ 5. So 20.39 rounds to _____.

5. Add the rounded numbers. _____ + _____ + _____ = _____

6. Marie's club traveled about _____ miles.

Use a calculator to check the estimate.

7. Is your estimate reasonable? _____

 Practice

Round each decimal to the nearest whole number.

1 56.31

2 31.86

3 29.51

4 85.4

_____   _____   _____   _____

Estimate each sum or difference. Check the estimate by using a calculator.

5
```
   75.42
 + 32.84
```

6
```
  116.82
  305.91
 + 12.75
```

7
```
   28.51
   36.31
 + 81.79
```

8
```
   59.2
 − 18.4
```

9
```
   93.21
 − 62.67
```

10
```
   67.91
 + 58.25
```

11
```
   71.01
 − 65.92
```

12
```
   57.18
 − 28.41
```

13
```
   41.23
 + 50.58
```

 14 Maria's family is going to visit relatives. They are driving 35.8 miles to her grandparents' house. After visiting there, they are driving 89.9 miles to Aunt Lucy's home. From Aunt Lucy's, they will drive 18.2 miles to see Uncle Manuel.

Estimate the number of miles they will travel on this trip. _____

Add the miles using a calculator. _____

Is your estimate reasonable? _____

15 Dan has a clothing budget of $60.00. He has found a hat for $12.98, some jeans for $22.45, a shirt for $19.75, and shoes for $36.50. Estimate which three items he can buy and then use a calculator to total the prices. Show your work. Is the total less than $60.00? _____

Short Response Question

16 Mel's dogs weigh 45.5 pounds, 34.9 pounds, and 56.2 pounds. He bought enough dog food for 2 weeks for a 70-pound dog. About how long will the food last for his dogs? Show your work. Check with a calculator.

Lesson 6.13 ▪ Greater than one—less than one

 Think About It

When can multiplication give you a product smaller than the number you started with?

 Here's How

1. When you multiply a number by 1, what is the product?

$5 \times 1 =$ _____
$88 \times 1 =$ _____

Rule: When you multiply a number by 1, the product is the number you started with.

2. When you multiply a number by a number greater than 1, is the product <u>greater than</u> or <u>less than</u> the number you started with?

$5 \times 2 =$ _____
$88 \times 2 =$ _____

Rule: When you multiply a number by a number greater than 1, the product is _____ than the number you started with.

3. When you multiply a number by a number less than 1, is the product <u>greater than</u> or <u>less than</u> the number you started with?

$88 \times \frac{1}{2} = 88 \times .5$
$= 44$
$44 < 88$

Rule: When you multiply a number by a number less than 1, the product is _____ than the number you started with.

 Practice

Circle the letter with the most reasonable answer.

1 $248 \times .25 =$

A 62
B 248
C 488
D None of the above

2 $42 \times \frac{1}{2} =$

F 84
G 42
H 21
J None of the above

3 $9 \times .3 =$

A 27
B 2.7
C 9
D None of the above

4 $1,500 \times 12 =$

F 1,500
G 989
H .989
J 18,000

5 12 × .75 =

A 127

B 89

C 9

D 75

6 138 × .65 =

F 381

G 138

H 89.7

J 8,970

7 1,999,999 × 3 =

A 5,999,997

B 621.8

C .59

D 1,999,999

8 67 × .38 =

F 25.46

G 67

H 380

J 91

9 85 × .37 = x

A x < 85

B x > 85

C x = 85

D None of these

10 2,349 × .75 =

F 23,497

G 1,761.75

H 2,349

J 7,500

11 9,999 × .15 = x

A x < 9,999

B x > 9,999

C x = 9,999

D None of these

12 649 × .9 =

F 649

G 5,484.1

H 584.1

J None of these

13 Ann walks to school each morning and takes the bus home. Her school is .65 miles from her house. She wants to know how many miles she walks in 5 days. When she multiplies 5 × .65, will she find she walks more than 5 miles or less than 5 miles?

Answer _____ **Why?** _____

14 Ramon's neighborhood has 7 streets, each .48 mile long. When Ramon multiplies .48 by 7 to find the total length of all the streets, will the product be more than 7 or less than 7?

Answer _____ **Why?** _____

Short Response Question

15 Hannah and Jesse are doing math homework together. They are figuring estimates for several problems. One of the problems is 874 × .67. Jesse's estimate is 58,000. Hannah's estimate is 580. Which estimate is reasonable? Explain your answer.

_____

_____

Lesson 6.14 ▪ Estimation strategies for multiplication and division

Think About It

Ken had 27 logs to divide between 3 fireplaces. Will there be more than 27 logs for each fireplace or less than 27 logs for each fireplace?

Here's How

1. When you divide a number by 1, what is the quotient? $27 \div 1 =$ ____

Rule: When you divide a number by 1, the quotient is the number you started with.

2. When you divide a number by a number greater than 1, is the quotient <u>greater</u> <u>than</u> or <u>less</u> <u>than</u> the number you started with?

$27 \div 3 =$ ____
$9 < 27$

Rule: When you divide a number by a number greater than 1, the product is _____ than the dividend.

3. When you divide a number by a number less than 1, is the quotient <u>greater</u> <u>than</u> or <u>less</u> <u>than</u> the number you started with?

$27 \div .25 = 108$
$108 > 27$

Rule: When you divide a number by a number less than 1, the product is _____ than the dividend.

Practice

Circle the letter with the most reasonable answer.

1 $350 \div .25$

A 1,400
B 350
C 140
D None of the above

2 $350 \div 25$

F 350
G 1,400
H 14
J None of the above

3 $9 \div .3$

A 30
B 3
C 6
D None of the above

4 128 ÷ .40

   A 32

   B 64

   C 400

   D 320

5 498 ÷ 22

   F 23

   G 2,490

   H 996

   J 1,992

6 335 ÷ .5

   A 67

   B 670

   C 6.09

   D 335

7 85 ÷ .37 = x

   F $x < 85$

   G $x > 85$

   H $x = 85$

   J None of these

8 2,349 ÷ 75

   A 31.32

   B 3,132

   C 2,349

   D 176,175

9 76 ÷ 1 = x

   F 75

   G 76

   H 77

   J 75

10 Alf is working on a jigsaw puzzle with three of his friends. The puzzle has 1,340 pieces. He needs to divide the pieces into 4 equal groups. Will each person have about 335 pieces or about 3,350 pieces? How do you know?

   Answer _____

11 Kyra's class has earned 1,275 points in a school-wide contest. Each student earned about the same number of points. There are 19 students in the class. Kyra says that each student earned about 70 points. Jason disagrees. He says that each student earned about 1,300 points. Whose estimate is the most reasonable? Why?

   Answer _____

Short Response Question

12 Keith and Paul are doing math homework together. They are doing estimates for several problems. One of the problems is 1,874 ÷ .39. Keith's estimate is 50. Paul's estimate is 4,800. Which student has the most reasonable estimate? Explain why.

_____

_____

Lesson 6.15 ▪ Predict outcomes

Think About It

You can use probability to help predict what the outcome of an experiment might be. In a paper bag containing blocks of different shapes, there is a square, a rectangle, a circle, and a triangle. Reach into the bag, take out a block and then return it to the bag. What shape will you pull out each time? What are the possible outcomes? How many different outcomes are there?

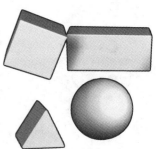

Here's How

Step 1 How many blocks are in the bag? _____

Are all the blocks the same shape? _____

Step 2 List the different shapes. _____

Step 3 There is an outcome every time you reach into the bag and take out a block. Name the possible outcomes each time you reach into the bag.

_____

Is it possible to have a hexagon block as an outcome? _____

How many different outcomes do you think are possible? _____

You would have to reach into the bag at least 4 times to get each shape at least once, but it might take more than 4 tries. It is equally probable that you will pick the square, the rectangle, the circle, or the rectangle. If another bag contained 2 squares, 1 rectangle, 1 circle, and 1 triangle, it would be more probable to pick a _____ as an outcome than any other shape.

Practice

1 Julie's mother prepared a basket of fruit to take on a picnic. The basket contains 1 pear, 2 apples, 1 orange, 1 banana, 1 grapefruit, and 1 tangerine.

If Julie picks a fruit without looking, is it more probable that she will pick an apple or a tangerine? _____

Name the possible different outcomes when Julie reaches into the basket of fruit.

_____

2 The sides of a cube are labeled A, B, C, D, E, and F.

How many outcomes are possible if the cube is rolled 1 time? _____

Name each outcome. _____

Would it be possible to have J as an outcome? _____

If you roll the cube 25 times, would the number of possible outcomes change?

_____

3 A box contains a slip of paper for each month of the year. Six students are drawing a slip from the box and then replacing it.

How many different outcomes are possible? _____

Is there any way to predict which month of the year the first student is most likely to draw?

_____

Short Response Question

Answer the questions using the spinner. Explain your answers.

4 What animal should go in the empty space for the spinner to have an equal chance of landing on each animal?

_____

How many outcomes are possible if you spin the spinner one time? Name each one.

_____

Is it possible to obtain a "cow" outcome?

_____

If the empty section pictured a cat, how would it change the outcomes?

_____

_____

Lesson 6.16 ▪ Certain and impossible events

 Think About It

Some events have no chance of occurring. We use the word **impossible** to describe these events. Some events must happen. We use the word **certain** to describe these events.

What is the probability that an egg will break if it is dropped on a cement floor—certain or impossible? What is the probability that someone will win a gold medal in the Olympic skating competition if they do not skate—certain or impossible?

 Here's How

Some events are certain.

Think: How likely is it that an egg will break when dropped on cement?

1. What do you know about eggs? Are they likely to break? _____

2. What do you know about cement? Is it a soft or a hard surface?

   _____

3. When something as fragile as an egg falls on a hard surface, it is _____ to break.

It is a certain event that an egg will break if it is dropped on a cement floor.

Some events are impossible.

Think: How likely is it that a person who does not skate will win an Olympic medal in skating?

1. Who enters the Olympic skating competition? _____

2. Can someone who cannot skate enter the contest? _____

3. Only someone entered in the competition can possibly win an Olympic medal.

It is an impossible event that someone who does not skate will win an Olympic medal in skating.

Practice

Answer certain *or* impossible *for each of the following questions.*

1 What is the probability that the Atlantic Ocean will be dry tomorrow morning? _____

2 What is the probability that the Atlantic Ocean will contain water tomorrow morning? _____

3 What is the probability that a fourth-grade student will become the president of the United States in the next election? _____

4 What is the probability that a car will run without fuel?  _____

5 What is the probability that this calendar year will include the month of November? _____

6 What is the probability of rolling a 2 on a number cube? _____

7 How likely is it that when you use this spinner it will land on 9? 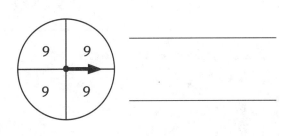 _____

8 How likely is it that this spinner will land on 3? _____

Extended Response Question

9 Describe one event that is certain to occur and one event that has no chance of occurring and explain why.

_____

_____

_____

_____

Lesson 6.17 ▪ Explain why a game is fair or unfair

Think About It

Haley and Justin are playing a game in which they use a spinner to determine how many spaces they can move. Will the game be fair or unfair if they both use Spinner A? Will the game be fair if Haley uses Spinner A and Justin uses Spinner B? Does fair mean that each player will get equal results?

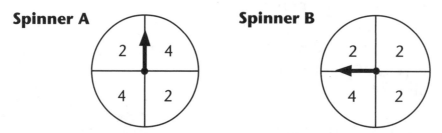

Spinner A **Spinner B**

Here's How

A Fair Spinner

1. Is the probability that Spinner A will land on 2 the same as the probability that it will land on 4? _____

The probability is equal because the area for 2 is the same as the area for 4.

2. The game will be _____ if Haley and Justin both use Spinner A.

Fair means that there is equal probability, not that there will be equal results.

An Unfair Spinner

1. Is the probability that Spinner B will land on 2 the same as the probability that it will land on 4? _____

The probability that Spinner B will land on 2 is not equal to the probability that it will land on 4 because the area for 2 is not equal to the area for 4.

2. It is more likely that Spinner B will land on _____ than on _____.

3. The game will be _____ if Haley uses Spinner A and Justin uses Spinner B.

Unfair means that there is not an equal probability.

Practice

Amy's fourth-grade class is divided into 2 teams, Team 1 and Team 2. A spinner determines which team takes a turn. Tell whether each spinner is fair or unfair.

1

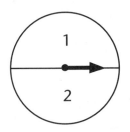

2

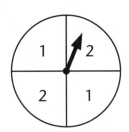

3

_____

4

5

6

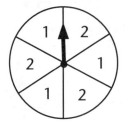

_____

7 Alisha's favorite board game uses a color cube. Players toss the cube. The player whose color shows on top gets the next turn. One side is red, one is blue, one is yellow, two are orange, and one is purple. Why would Kerry think the game is unfair?

_____

Short Response Question

8 Bill and Harriet play a game each morning to decide who will ride in the front seat of the car on the way to school. Dad draws a slip of paper from a sack and the person whose name is on the slip gets the front seat. There are a total of 10 slips in the sack—5 slips with Bill's name and 5 slips with Harriet's name. Is this game fair or unfair? Explain your answer.

_____

_____

Lesson 6.18 • Collect statistical data

> **READY REFERENCE**
>
> **data** gathered facts or information
>
> **poll** a survey of the public or of a sample of public opinion to acquire information
>
> **prediction** a statement about what might happen

 Think About It

Predictions can be made from data. Data can be collected from newspapers, magazines, and polls. Mrs. Wright asked Julie to predict what game the class will choose to play during recess. What data does Julie need to collect? How can she gather this information?

 Here's How

What data is needed?

1. Julie needs to know the class's favorite _____ in order to make a reasonable prediction.

How might the data be collected?

2. Julie decides to take a poll of the class. She lists each student's favorite game on the board in a chart similar to the one below.

Baseball	Soccer	Basketball
ℍℍ /	ℍℍ ℍℍ	///

3. Which game do most of the students like best? _____

4. Julie predicts that the class will choose to play _____ during recess.

🔑 Practice

1 Roberto's local newspaper published the following data about the current baseball season.
Which team do you predict will win first place?

_____

Baseball

mondbacks 7, Mets 1

AB	R	H	BI	BB	SO	Avg.
3	1	2	0	1	0	.333
4	0	0	0	0	0	.222
0	0	0	1	1	0	.375
0	1	0	0	2	0	.222
0	0	0	2	0	0	.333
0	0	0	0	1	0	.000
0	0	0	0	0	0	.000
0	1	0	0	1	0	.250
			0	0	1	.250
1	0	0	0	2		.286
0	0	0	0	01	.000
0	0	0	00		—
0	0	0	1		.000
0	0	0	0		—
0	1	.000
5	7
SO	Avg
3	.111
0	.375
	500
5

Summitville Summer Season

Team	Games Played	Won	Lost
Diamond Backs	20	18	2
Aces	21	12	9
Clubs	20	2	18

BIG 12

Missouri at Colorada (by 11), Noon
Iowa St. at Nbraska (by 30), 7 pm
Kansas at Kansas St. (by 29), 2 pm
Texas Tech at Oklahoma St. (by 3)

2 A magazine article reports that the sales of tennis shoes have increased every year for the past ten years. Based on these statistics, what do you predict will happen to the sales of tennis shoes this year?

_____

_____

3 Mei's newspaper reports that 3 out of 5 babies born in her town are boys. Her new brother or sister will be born next month. After reading the article she predicts that she will have a new _____.

4 Bo asked each family in his apartment building to name their favorite dessert. He put the data into a chart. A new family moved into his building. Bo predicted that their favorite dessert would be _____.

Pie	Cake	Cookies	Pudding
THL III	THL THL THL THL	THL I	THL

Short Response Question

5 A newspaper published information about last year's community events. Based on this data, which month do you predict will be the busiest this year? Explain your answer.

_____

_____

_____

Month	Events
January	2
February	3
March	1
April	3
May	2
June	4
July	4
August	3
September	5
October	3
November	4
December	8

Lesson 6.19 ▪ Predict with spinners

🔑 Think About It

You do not know what the outcome will be when you spin a spinner, roll a number cube, or pick something out of a group of items without looking. But you can predict the probability of getting a particular outcome and the result. If you spin the spinner, can you predict where it will land?

🔑 Here's How

Step 1 Gather information about the sections.

    1. How many sections does the spinner have? _____

    2. Are the sections equal? _____

    3. How many sections are labeled A? _____

    4. How many sections are labeled B? _____

    5. How many sections are labeled C? _____

Step 2 Determine the probabilities.

    6. The probability of the spinner landing on A is 3 out of 10.

    7. The probability of the spinner landing on B is 3 out of _____.

    8. The probability of the spinner landing on C is _____ out of _____.

    9. Is the probability the same that the spinner will land on A or C? _____ No, it is less likely to land on A because 3 is less than 4, or it is more likely to land on C because 4 is more than _____.

    10. It is equally likely to land on A or B because 3 = _____.

    11. It is more likely to land on C than on B because 4 is _____ than 3.

Step 3 Predict where the spinner will land.

    12. You can predict that the spinner is more likely to land on _____.

🔑 Practice

*Fill in the blanks with **more likely, less likely,** or **equally likely.***

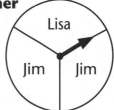

1 The spinner is _____ to land on A or B.

2 The spinner is _____ to land on B than C.

3 The spinner is _____ to land on C than A.

4 The spinner is _____ to land on A than C.

5 The spinner is _____ to land on C than B.

6 Dad wants someone to be responsible for keeping the car clean while he is away on a business trip. Jim and Lisa each designed a spinner for their dad to use to decide who will get the job. Predict who will get the job with Lisa's spinner and who will get the job with Jim's spinner. Explain your answers.

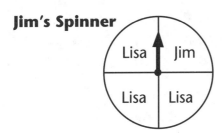

Jim's Spinner   **Lisa's Spinner**

_____

_____

Short Response Question

7 Nine blocks are all the same size, but they are different colors. Four blocks are red, 3 blocks are green, 1 block is yellow, and 1 block is purple. If you reach into the bag of blocks without looking, what is the probability that you will pick green?

Answer _____ out of _____

What color do you predict you would most likely pick? _____
Explain your answer.

_____

_____

Lesson 6.20 ▪ Unbiased random samples

> **READY REFERENCE**
> **unbiased random sample** a set in which every member has an equal chance
> of being chosen

 Think About It

What is your school's favorite game? If you ask
the students in the Chess Club to name their
favorite game, could you predict what their
answer might be?

 Here's How

How would you find out your school's favorite game?

1. You could ask every student in school to name their favorite game and tally
   the results.

   Members of the Chess Club would most likely pick chess, so they
   would not be an unbiased random sample. In other words, you could
   predict what their answer might be.

2. You could gather information from an unbiased random sample of the
   students to get a quick answer.

   Have each student in the school write their favorite game on a slip of
   paper and place the slip in a box. Draw 42 slips from the box without
   looking. Since you cannot predict what the answer might be, this is an
   unbiased random sample. Thirty students chose playing cards, 5
   students chose checkers, and 7 students chose chess. From this
   unbiased random sample, you can predict that your school's favorite
   game is _____.

 Practice

For each problem, circle the letter that represents an unbiased random sample.

1 What is your class's favorite kind of cookie?

A Every student in your class who is
eating a chocolate chip cookie at lunch

C Every student who is eating at
least two oatmeal cookies at lunch

B Every third student in your class

D None of the above

2 What is your school's favorite sports team?

F The baseball team   **H** The basketball team

G The soccer team   **J** None of the above

3 There are 12 marbles. Six are black, 3 are blue, and 3 are purple.

A Place the marbles on a table and pick one while looking at them.

B Place the marbles on a table and ask a friend whose favorite color is purple to pick one.

C Place the marbles on a table and pick one without looking.

D None of the above

Fill in the blanks.

4 A grocery store wants to find out which soap its customers like best.

Part A A questionnaire is given to every customer who has *Bubble Soap* in his or her shopping cart. What soap do you predict will be their favorite? _____ Is this an unbiased random sample? _____

Part B A questionnaire is given to every other customer as they leave the checkout counter. Can you predict what soap will be their favorite? _____ Is this an unbiased random sample? _____

Part C Fifty-eight questionnaires are given to every other customer. Thirty-eight like *Very Clean Soap* the best, 10 like *Scrub Soap* the best, and 10 like *Rosebud Soap* the best. What soap is most likely the favorite of the grocery store's customers? _____

Short Response Question

5 Your local television station wants to know your community's favorite program. There are 100 houses in your community. All of them have at least one television. Describe how you would conduct an unbiased random sample of your community.

_____

_____

_____

Lesson 6.21 ▪ How many ways can an event occur?

🔑 Think About It

In order to determine the probability of a simple event, it is necessary to know the number of ways that the event can occur. If you have a bag of cookies containing 1 chocolate chip cookie, 1 oatmeal cookie, and 1 sugar cookie, how many ways can you get an oatmeal cookie? What is the probability that you will select the oatmeal cookie if you reach into the bag without looking?

🔑 Here's How

Step 1 How many cookies are in the bag? _____

Step 2 How many oatmeal cookies are in the bag? There is _____ oatmeal cookie in the bag, so there is 1 chance of getting an oatmeal cookie.

Step 3 What is the probability you will get the oatmeal cookie when you reach into the bag?

The probability is _____ out of 3.

Step 4 If you do not pick the oatmeal cookie the first time, there will be 2 cookies left in the bag. If you reach into the bag again, the probability of picking the oatmeal cookie is 1 out of _____.

To find the probability of a simple event, you must determine the number of ways the event can occur and the number of different outcomes that are possible.

🔑 Practice

For each problem, circle the letter that represents the number of ways the event can occur.

1 How many ways can you pick a grape ice pop from a box that contains 3 cherry, 3 grape, 3 raspberry, and 3 strawberry ice pops?

A 12 **B** 6 **C** 4 **D** 3

2 A letter cube has one A, two B's, one C, and two D's. How many ways can the cube land on D?

F 6 **G** 4 **H** 2 **J** None of the answers

3 There are 12 marbles in a bag. Six are black, 3 are blue, and 3 are purple. How many ways can you pick a purple marble?

A 3 **B** 12 **C** 6 **D** None of these

4 Using the bag of marbles in Problem 3, what is the probability that you will pick a black marble? _____

5 Joseph's family wants to go to a movie on Saturday. The theater has 8 screens. Two cartoon features, 1 animal adventure, 2 mysteries, 1 sports story, 1 foreign film, and 1 love story are showing. How many ways can his family see a mystery? _____ What is the probability that his family will see a mystery? _____

Short Response Question

6 Marianne's mother has 5 cookbooks that each contain a recipe for chocolate chip cookies. Two recipes have pecans in the list of ingredients.

Part A How many different recipes for chocolate chip cookies does Marianne have to choose from? _____ Explain your answer.

_____

_____

_____

_____

Part B How many ways can Marianne get a recipe that includes pecans?

A 2 **B** 5 **C** 3 **D** 1

Part C What is the probability that Marianne will pick a recipe with pecans? _____ Explain your answer.

_____

_____

_____

Lesson 6.22 ▪ Use fractional notation to express the probability of an occurrence

> **READY REFERENCE**
> **probability** how likely something is to happen
> **ratio** a comparison of one number to another

 Think About It

Did you ever flip a coin with a friend? A coin has two sides, so two things can happen. The coin can come up heads or tails. The probability of picking correctly is 1 out of 2.

 Here's How

At a school picnic, five kinds of lunches are being served. They are hot dogs, baked turkey, cold cuts, tuna salad, and chicken salad. You have an equal chance of getting any of the lunches. Your favorite food is chicken salad. What is the probability that you will get chicken salad for lunch?

Step 1 Count the number of possible outcomes.

1. How many kinds of lunches are being served? _____

Step 2 Find how many chances you have of getting the outcome you want.

2. How many of the lunches have chicken salad? _____

3. How many of the lunches contain something other than chicken salad? _____

Step 3 Write the probability as numbers in a ratio.

4. $P = \dfrac{\text{number of lunches with chicken salad}}{\text{number of different lunches being served}} = $ _____

5. The probability of getting chicken salad for lunch is 1 in _____ chances.

🔑 Practice

 1 A box of 15 pencils contains 4 red pencils, 3 blue pencils, 5 green pencils, and 3 purple pencils. You can have 1 pencil. Write the probability for getting each color as a ratio.   red _____   blue _____
green _____   purple _____

What color pencil are you most likely to get? _____

2 There were 30 tickets purchased for a drawing at school. Of these, Marta bought 3 and Brent bought 7. What is the probability that either Marta or Brent will win the prize?

A $\frac{3}{30}$ **B** $\frac{10}{30}$ **C** $\frac{3}{7}$ **D** $\frac{7}{30}$

3 You toss a cube numbered 1-6 and it comes up 5. What is the probability that it will come up 5 on your next toss?

F $\frac{1}{100}$ **G** $\frac{1}{2}$ **H** $\frac{1}{3}$ **J** $\frac{1}{6}$

 4 You must choose one of the following circles from a box without looking.

What is the probability that you will choose this one?

A $\frac{1}{9}$ **B** $\frac{2}{9}$ **C** $\frac{4}{9}$ **D** $\frac{7}{9}$

Short Response Question
Write the probabilities as numbers in a ratio.
Show your work and explain your answers.

5 In the game you are playing, you are allowed to spin the spinner one time.

Part A What is the probability of getting a number? _____

_____

Part B What is the probability of getting a black space? _____

_____

Part C What is the probability of getting the number 5? _____

_____

Lesson 6.23 ▪ Pictures, lists, and tree diagrams

⚷ Think About It

Organizing data can help in determining the probability of a simple event. Drawing a picture or making a list from a tree diagram helps organize the data.

⚷ Here's How

Use pictures.

Micah has a bag of marbles. It contains 4 striped marbles, 2 black marbles, and 2 white marbles. What is the probability that Janet will choose a white marble when she reaches into the bag without looking?

1. Draw a picture. Show the striped marbles together, the black marbles together, and the white marbles together.

2. Count the items in the picture. There are _____ marbles.

3. Count the white marbles. There are _____ white marbles.

4. The probability of choosing a white marble is _____ out of _____.

Make a list from a tree diagram.

Joseph's team is ordering uniforms. Their choices are navy or purple. The letters can be white, red, or green. What is the probability they will pick a navy uniform with white letters?

1. Draw a tree diagram.

navy uniform — white ——— navy and white
— red ——— navy and red
— green ——— navy and green

purple uniform — white ——— purple and white
— red ——— purple and red
— green ——— purple and green

2. Make a list of the possible choices: navy–white, navy–red, navy–green, purple–white, purple–red, purple–green.

3. How many possible choices are there? _____

4. The probability of choosing a navy uniform with white letters is _____ out of _____.

Practice

Draw a tree diagram and make a list to find the answer.

1 An art assignment requires the use of a black or a blue pen and one red, purple, or green marker. What is the probability that Michael will choose a black pen and a green marker?

_____

2 Alisha has a choice of vanilla or chocolate ice cream. She can choose one topping. The available toppings are strawberry, hot fudge, caramel, and blackberry. What is the probability that she will choose vanilla ice cream with hot fudge topping?

_____

Draw a picture to find the answer.

3 Amy has a box of shapes—4 squares, 3 circles, 2 triangles, and 3 rectangles. What is the probability she will pick a square if she reaches into the box without looking?

_____

Short Response Question

4 Jill is choosing an outfit to wear to visit her grandmother. She has 4 T-shirts—purple, blue, red, and green. She can wear a T-shirt with either a skirt or pants. What is the probability she will choose a purple T-shirt with a skirt? Draw a picture or create a tree diagram, then make a list. Explain your work.

_____

_____

Directions
Use a separate piece of paper to show your work.

1 Use the thermometer to find the temperature and round it to the nearest ten.

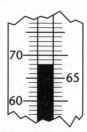

temperature _____°

rounded _____°

2 Use front-end estimation to find a high and low estimate, then solve the problem.

High estimate _____   8,657

Low estimate _____   − 1,213

Is your answer reasonable?_____

3 A recipe calls for $2\frac{3}{4}$ c flour and $3\frac{1}{4}$ c sugar. If the ingredients are rounded to the nearest cup, how much of each will be used?

A 3 c flour and 4 c sugar
B 2 c flour and 3 c sugar
C 3 c flour and 3 c sugar
D 4 c flour and 4 c sugar

4 A number cube has been tossed 6 times. What is the probability that 3 will be on top on the next toss?

F $\frac{1}{6}$ **H** $\frac{1}{7}$

G $\frac{3}{6}$ **J** $\frac{3}{7}$

5 Eight people are working on a puzzle with 4,550 pieces. If the pieces are divided evenly, will each person get about 500 pieces, about 50 pieces, or about 5,000 pieces?

Answer   about _____ pieces

6 What vehicle should go in the empty space for the spinner to have an equal chance of landing on each one?

A boat
B car
C truck
D airplane

7 A poll shows that 8 students prefer brownies, 3 prefer pie, 4 prefer cake, and 15 prefer ice cream. What do you predict a student will order for dessert?

F pie   **H** brownies
G cake   **J** ice cream

8 There are 4 red marbles, 2 purple marbles, and 3 blue marbles in a bag. What is the probability that you will pick a red marble from the bag without looking?

A 4 out of 4   **C** 4 out of 9
B 1 out of 9   **D** 9 out of 10

Lesson 7.1 ▪ Number patterns and sequences

 Think About It

Some animals can form new organisms by splitting. Certain worms stretch until they split in half. Each half becomes a new worm! Suppose a worm splits in half. Each of the two new worms then splits in half. If this continues five times, how many worms would there be?

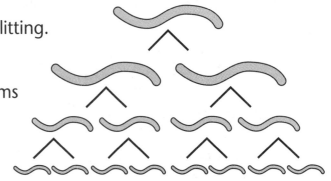

Here's How

Step 1 Make a diagram.

1. Count the number of worms in each row of the diagram. Row 1 has one worm. Row 2 has _____ worms. Row 3 has four worms. Row 4 has _____ worms.

2. Write the numbers in a line: 1, _____ , 4, _____ .

3. Recognize the pattern.

➤ Look at the first and second numbers. They are 1 and 2. Think about what you do to the first number to get the second number. You multiply 1 by _____ to get 2.

➤ Look at the second and third numbers. They are 2 and _____ . Think about what you do to the second number to get the third number. You multiply 2 by 2 to get _____ .

➤ Look at the third and fourth numbers. They are _____ and 8. Think about what you do to the third number to get the fourth number. You multiply _____ by 2 to get _____ .

Step 2 Describe the pattern.

4. Explain what actions are being done to each number. You multiply each number by _____ to get the next number.

Step 3 Extend the pattern.

5. Find the next two numbers in this pattern.

➤ Think $8 \times 2 = 16$, so the fifth number is 16.

➤ Think $16 \times 2 = 32$, so the sixth number is 32.

After the worms split 5 times, there would be 32 worms!

 Practice

Fill in the blanks to complete the pattern.

1 1, 6, 11, ____ , ____

2 52, 48, 44, ____ , ____

3 1, 3, ____ , 27, ____ , 243

4 13, 15, 19, 25, ____ , ____

5 100, 95, 85, 70, ____ , ____

6 8, 9, 11, ____ , 18, ____

7 63, 61, 66, 64, ____ , ____

8 23, 31, 28, 36, ____ , ____

9 24 , 29, 27, 32, 30, ____ , ____

10 16, 8, 32, 16, ____ , ____

11 An elevator was on the first floor. It went up 4 floors, and then it went down 2 floors. It went up 4 more floors and then down 2 floors. On what floor is the elevator?

_____

12 On the first day of the month, a school cafeteria sold 85 cartons of milk. On the second day, 92 cartons were sold. On the third day, 99 cartons were sold. If this pattern continues, how many cartons were sold on the fifth day of the month?

_____

Short Response Question

13 The owner of Al's Diner keeps a record of the number of lunch specials sold daily. The table below shows results for part of a week. Use your understanding of patterns to complete the chart. Explain how you solved the problem.

Specials	Monday	Tuesday	Wednesday	Thursday	Friday	Saturday
#1	28	32	36		44	
#2	13	16		22		28

_____

_____

_____

Lesson 7.2 ▪ Repeated patterns

🔑 Think About It

You watch as your friend makes a bracelet. She places two round beads on a wire. Then she adds a square bead, a diamond bead, and two more round beads. Your friend is called to the telephone. As she leaves the room, she hands you the wire. "Add more beads in the same pattern," she says. But you don't know what pattern she is using! How will you identify this pattern?

🔑 Here's How

Step 1 Recognize the pattern.

1. There are _____ different-shaped beads on the wire.

2. First there are two _____ beads, then one _____ bead, then one _____ bead, then two _____ beads.

3. The first and second beads are the same shape as the _____ and _____ beads. So, the pattern is only _____ beads long.

4. The pattern is _____.

Step 2 Extend the pattern.

5. The last two beads are both _____.

6. In the pattern, they are followed by a _____.

7. It is followed by _____.

🔑 Practice

Name the next five beads in the pattern.

1. White – Blue – Blue – Red – White – Blue _____

2. Green – White – Green – Blue – Green – White _____

3. Gold – Silver – Silver – Gold – Silver _____

4. White – White – Red – White – White – Blue – White – White – Red

_____

5. Blue – Gold – Blue – Blue – Gold – Gold – Blue – Gold _____

6   Orange – Orange – Yellow – Green – Orange – Orange _____

7   Silver – Silver – Red – Silver – Red – Silver – Silver _____

8   Gold – Green – Green – Green – Gold – Gold – Green _____

Read each problem carefully. Draw a picture to find the pattern. Use the pattern to find the answer.

9   Ruth will use 20 beads to make a bracelet. She is using a pattern of 2 red beads, 1 white bead, and 2 blue beads. How many white beads will be on Ruth's bracelet?

_____

10   Kim is making a necklace for her sister. There will be 40 beads on the necklace. Kim is following a pattern of 2 silver beads, and 3 gold beads. How many times will this pattern occur on the necklace?

_____

Draw the next five shapes in each pattern.

11   ▲ , ▲ , ■ , ■ , ● , _____

12   ● , ◆ , ■ , ▲ , ▲ , _____

13   ■ , ■ , ■ , ● , ▲ , ● , _____

Short Response Question

14   Dixie made bracelets on Monday, Thursday, and Sunday. If this pattern continues, what are the next three days Dixie will make bracelets? Explain how you found your answer.

_____

_____

_____

Lesson 7.3 ▪ Design patterns

> **READY REFERENCE**
> **pattern** a series of items or actions that happen in a specific order
> **order** the characteristic that items in a pattern have in common
> **sequence** the order in which the items in a pattern are arranged

 Think About It

Patterns are everywhere in the world. Special relationships between items make patterns. How often these relationships happen affect the pattern's order, or sequence. Look at the pattern below. What is the next shape in this pattern?

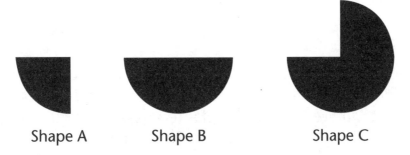

Shape A   Shape B   Shape C

 Here's How

Compare Shape A and Shape B.

1. What part of a circle is shown in Shape A? ___$\frac{1}{4}$ or one quarter___

2. What part of a circle is shown in Shape B? _____

3. What was done to Shape A to form Shape B? _____

Compare Shape B and Shape C.

4. What part of a circle is shown in Shape C? _____

5. What was done to Shape B to form Shape C?

_____

6. What relationship exists between these two shapes?

_____

7. Draw Shape D.

🔑 **Practice**

Draw the next item in the pattern.

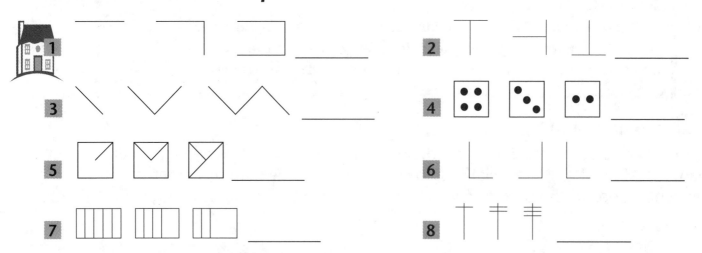

9 Jon is planting flowers in his square-shaped garden. On Monday, he planted flowers along the top edge of the garden. On Tuesday, he planted flowers along the left edge of the garden. On Wednesday, he planted flowers along the bottom edge of the garden. Where will Jon plant flowers on Thursday?

_____

Short Response Question

10 Adam cut a pie into 8 slices. His family ate two slices. His friends ate two slices. He gave two slices to his neighbor. Draw three shapes to show how the amount of pie changed. Then draw a fourth shape to show how much of the pie is left. Explain how you found your answer.

_____

_____

_____

Lesson 7.4 ▪ Use symbols <, >, ≤, and ≥

> **READY REFERENCE**
>
> **compare** examine two or more numbers to see which is greater or lesser
>
> **order** put three or more numbers in order from greatest to least, or least to greatest
>
> < symbol that stands for *less than*
>
> ≤ symbol that stands for *less than or equal to*
>
> > symbol that stands for *greater than*
>
> ≥ symbol that stands for *greater than or equal to*

 Think About It

Luke, Alma, Rico, and Jill belong to a baseball card club. Luke has 378 cards. Alma has 389 cards. Rico has 218 cards. Jill has 216 cards. How could you determine which club member has the greatest number of cards? How could you determine which club member has the least number of cards?

Here's How

Step 1 Compare the numbers two at a time. Start from the left. Compare until you find digits that are different.

   1. Which two digits are different? _____

   2. Which of these digits is greater? _____

   3. Which of the numbers is greater? _____

378 and 389

Step 2 Compare the next two numbers. Start from the left. Compare until you find digits that are different.

   4. Which two digits are different? _____

   5. Which of these digits is greater? _____

   6. Which of the numbers is greater? _____

218 and 216

Step 3 Use the symbols to order the numbers from greatest to least.

   7. Write the four numbers in order from greatest to least, using the correct symbol. _____

   8. Who has the greatest number of cards? _____

   9. Who has the least number of cards? _____

Practice

Compare the numbers. Write the correct symbol in each blank.

1 187 ___ 871

2 541 ___ 456

3 602 ___ 621

4 1,907 ___ 1,909

5 7,235 ___ 7,253

6 381 ___ 3,800

7 6,885 ___ 6,888

8 4,714 ___ 4,741

9 9,114 ___ 9,111

10 Marty has 336 cards. Don has 8 fewer cards than Marty. Rhea has 12 more cards than Marty. Who has the greatest number of cards? Who has the least number of cards? Show your work.

11 Andy has 117 album pages filled with cards. Marguerite's card collection fills 12 fewer pages. Chao's collection fills 8 fewer pages. All the pages hold the same number of cards. Who has the greatest number of cards? Who has the least number of cards?

Extended Response Question

12 Michael has 245 cards. Zack has 217 cards. Rudy had 221 cards yesterday. He will buy 3 packs of cards today. Each pack has either 8 or 10 cards. After Rudy gets his new packs, how would you order the boys from greatest to least number of cards? How could you use symbols to show this relationship? Explain your answer.

Lesson 7.5 ▪ At most and at least

> **READY REFERENCE**
> **dividend** the number to be divided
> **divisor** the number by which another number is divided
> **quotient** the answer in division
> **remainder** the number left over after dividing

 Think About It

Juan works at the Ice Cream Shop. He has to place 160 cones into 3 containers. Each container should hold the same number of cones. At most, how many cones can Juan put into each container? How many cones will be left over?

 Here's How

Step 1 Write the problem. 160 ÷ 3 = ?

Step 2 Solve the problem. Show your work below.

At most, how many cones should Juan put in each container? _____
How many cones will be left over? _____

 Practice

Read each problem. Write your answers on the lines.

1 Pat had 122 stickers to separate equally into 4 albums. At most, how many stickers can she put in each album?

Part A Write the division problem. _____

Part B Solve the problem. What is the answer? _____

Part C At most, how many stickers can Pat put in each album? _____
How many stickers will be left over? _____

2 Jon is reading a book about New York State history for class. The book has 117 pages. At least, how many pages must he read to finish the book at the end of 9 days? Show your work.

Part A What division sentence should Jon use to answer the question? _____

Part B Solve the problem. What is the answer? _____

Part C At least, how many pages should Jon read each day in order to finish the book in 9 days? _____

3 Clyde has 211 baseball cards. He plans to divide the cards evenly among 6 containers. At most, how many cards should Clyde put in each container?

Part A What division sentence should Clyde use to answer this question? _____

Part B Solve the problem. What is the answer? _____

Part C At most, how many cards should Clyde put in each container? _____ How many cards will be left over? _____

Short Response Question

4 When a question includes the words at most, do you include the remainder as part of the answer? Explain your answer.

_____

_____

_____

Lesson 7.6 ▪ Describing division

> **READY REFERENCE**
> **division** finding the quotient of a dividend and a divisor
> **dividend** a number to be divided
> **divisor** the number by which a dividend is divided
> **quotient** the number that results by dividing

Think About It

How many names do you answer to? You can be called by your first name. You can be called by your first and last name. Perhaps you have a nickname, too. All these names refer to the same thing—YOU! There are different ways that you can represent division facts, too. Can you name three different ways of showing 18 divided by 3?

Here's How

Identify the dividend and divisor in 18 divided by 3.

1. What number is being divided? _____ This is the dividend.

2. What number is being divided into the dividend? _____ This is the divisor.

Use a division sign to write the division fact.

1. Write the problem in this order: dividend, division sign, divisor.

_____

Write the division fact as a fraction.

1. Write the dividend over the divisor. _____

Use ⟌ to write the division fact.

1. Write the divisor. Then write the dividend under the line. _____

Practice

Circle __all__ the correct answers.

1 21 divided by 7

   A $\frac{7}{21}$ **B** $21\overline{)7}$

   C $21 \div 7$ **D** $\frac{21}{7}$

2 56 divided by 8

   F $\frac{56}{8}$ **G** $8 \div 56$

   H $8\overline{)56}$ **J** $56\overline{)8}$

3 36 divided by 9

  A $\frac{9}{36}$ **B** $9\overline{)36}$

  C $\frac{36}{9}$ **D** $9 \div 36$

4 100 divided by 10

  F $10 \div 100$ **G** $100 \div 10$

  H $100\overline{)10}$ **J** $10\overline{)100}$

5 72 divided by 8

  A $8\overline{)72}$ **B** $72\overline{)8}$

  C $\frac{72}{8}$ **D** $8 \div 72$

6 45 divided by 5

  F $45\overline{)5}$ **G** $5\overline{)45}$

  H $5 \div 45$ **J** $\frac{45}{5}$

Write the division fact for each problem three different ways.

7 Mia baked 12 brownies. She will divide the brownies evenly into three containers.

_____

8 Peter bought 64 apples. He will put them in bags of 8.

_____

9 There are five people in the Will family. Mrs. Will bought 15 juice boxes to divide evenly among the members of her family.

_____

Short Response Question

10 Tim has 42 stickers. He wants to divide them evenly among 6 friends. Tim wrote this division fact to determine how many stickers to give each person: $\frac{6}{42}$. Did he write the division fact the correct way? Explain your answer.

_____

_____

_____

Lesson 7.7 ▪ Describe number sequences

> **READY REFERENCE**
> **pattern** a series of items or actions that happen in a specific order
> **sequence** the order in which the items in a pattern are arranged

 Think About It

Are any walls in your home covered with wallpaper? If so, you look at a pattern every day. The designs on the wallpaper form a pattern. Some patterns are made up of numbers rather than designs. The numbers are arranged in a special sequence. Here is one number sequence: 1, 3, 6, 10 . . . Can you tell what the next two numbers of this sequence will be?

 Here's How

Step 1 Compare the first and second numbers.

    1. What is the first number of the sequence? _____

    2. What is the second number of the sequence? _____

    3. What was done to the first number to get the second number?

    _____

Step 2 Compare the second and third numbers.

    4. What is the third number? _____

    5. What was done to the second number to get the third number?

    _____

Step 3 Compare the third and fourth numbers.

    6. What is the fourth number? _____

    7. What was done to the third number to get the fourth number?

    _____

Step 4 Identify the pattern.

    8. What pattern is used to form this number sequence?

    _____

    9. What are the next two numbers? _____

🔑 Practice

Identify the pattern and write the next numbers in the sequence.

1 3, 4, 6, 9, _____ , _____ , _____ , _____ , _____ , _____

2 18, 13, 9, 6, _____ , _____

3 1, 2, 3, 5, _____ , _____ , _____ , _____ , _____ , _____

4 20, 17, 14, 11, _____ , _____ , _____

5 3, 7, 11, 15, _____ , _____ , _____ , _____ , _____ , _____

6 1, 2, 4, 8, _____ , _____ , _____ , _____ , _____ , _____

7 35, 30, 25, 20, _____ , _____ , _____ , _____

8 49, 42, 35, 28, _____ , _____ , _____ , _____ , _____ , _____

9 5, 10, 20, 35, _____ , _____ , _____ , _____ , _____ , _____

10 33, 41, 49, 57, _____ , _____ , _____ , _____ , _____ , _____

11 100, 95, 85, 70, _____ , _____ , _____

12 Jake exercised on June 1, 4, 7, and 10. If Jake keeps this schedule, what are the dates of the next two days he will exercise?

_____

13 Paula delivered newspapers on April 3, 7, 10, and 14. If Paula keeps this schedule, what are the dates of the next two days she will deliver newspapers?

_____

Short Response Question

14 Hannah practiced the piano on September 3, 6, 9, and 12. If she keeps this schedule, will Hannah practice on September 30? Explain how you found your answer.

_____

_____

_____

Lesson 7.8 ▪ Investigate relationships

 Think About It

When you were younger, did you play with blocks? If so, you probably used the blocks to make something. When you were finished, you would take it apart and start all over again. You can do the same thing when you solve math problems. You can use addition to build a number sentence like 8 + 7 = 15. Do you know how to undo this sentence?

 Here's How

Addition and subtraction

Undo 8 + 7 = 15 with subtraction. Turn the sentence around, and replace + with −. Write this new sentence: 15 − 7 = _____

Addition and multiplication

Use multiplication to find the sum of 3 + 3 + 3 + 3.
One factor is the addend that is repeated. What is this number? _____

The other factor is how many times the addend is repeated.
What is this number? _____
Write the multiplication fact. _____

Use division to undo multiplication.

Find the dividend and the divisor in 4 × 3 = 12. The product of the multiplication fact is the dividend. One of the factors is the divisor.

Write the division fact. _____
Divide to find the quotient. Compare this quotient with the multiplication fact. The quotient in the division problem is the _____ in the multiplication problem.

Division is also related to subtraction. Use subtraction to find 15 ÷ 3.

Subtract the divisor from the dividend. Continue subtracting over and over again until you get 0. 15 − 3 − _____ To find the quotient, count the number of times you subtracted. This is the quotient.

Write the division fact. _____

 **Practice**

Undo addition with subtraction. Write a subtraction fact on the line.

1 $8 + 12 = 20$ **2** $15 + 11 = 26$ **3** $29 + 6 = 35$

_____   _____   _____

Undo multiplication with division. Write a division fact on the line.

4 $9 \times 8 = 72$ **5** $6 \times 7 = 42$ **6** $4 \times 12 = 48$

_____   _____   _____

Write the related multiplication fact on the line.

7 $8 + 8 + 8 + 8$ **8** $6 + 6 + 6 + 6 + 6$ **9** $2 + 2 + 2$

_____   _____   _____

 10 Write the subtraction sentences you would use to find the quotient of $27 \div 9$.

_____

Short Response Question

11 **Part A** Ron wrote that the sum of 34 and 21 is 53. Explain how Ron can use subtraction to check his answer. Is he correct? Explain your answer.

_____

_____

Part B Explain how Ron can use subtraction to find $63 \div 7$.

_____

_____

Lesson 7.9 ▪ Relate fractional notation to decimals

> **READY REFERENCE**
>
> **fraction** a number that names a part of a whole
>
> **decimal** a number with one or more places to the right of the decimal point; the numbers to the right of the decimal point name part of a whole

🔑 Think About It

Mia has 10 stickers. She put 7 stickers on her books. Mia wrote the decimal 0.7 to represent the stickers she used. She said, "I used seven tenths of my stickers." How can she write this amount as a fraction?

🔑 Here's How

Write tenths.

1 2 3 4 5 6 7 8 9 10

Fraction: $\frac{7}{10}$

Decimal: 0.7

1. The fraction $\frac{7}{10}$ and the decimal 0.7 are read as *seven tenths.*

2. Do $\frac{7}{10}$ and 0.7 name the same part? _____

Write hundredths.

Fraction: $\frac{5}{100}$

Decimal: 0.05

1. The fraction _____ and the decimal _____ are read as _____ *hundredths.*

2. Do $\frac{5}{100}$ and 0.05 name the same part? _____

Write thousandths.

1. Do $\frac{734}{1,000}$ and 0.734 name the same part? _____

2. The fraction _____ and the decimal _____ are read as _____.

Equivalent fractions and decimals

 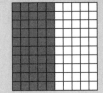

Fraction: $\frac{5}{10}$ or 0.5 = $\frac{50}{100}$ or 0.50

1. Do all the fractions and decimals name the same part? _____

 **Practice**

Write each decimal as a fraction.

1 0.4 _____

2 0.57 _____

3 0.409 _____

4 0.29 _____

5 0.726 _____

6 0.085 _____

7 0.013 _____

8 0.605 _____

Write each fraction as a decimal.

9 $\frac{3}{10}$ _____

10 $\frac{52}{100}$ _____

11 $\frac{497}{1,000}$ _____

12 $\frac{8}{10}$ _____

13 $\frac{117}{1,000}$ _____

14 $\frac{29}{100}$ _____

15 $\frac{755}{1,000}$ _____

16 $\frac{46}{100}$ _____

Write yes or no to tell if the decimals and fractions are equivalent.

17 0.3; 0.30

18 0.10; 0.1

19 $\frac{8}{10}$; 0.08

20 $\frac{87}{100}$; 0.8

_____

_____

_____

_____

 21 Rico has 100 sheets of construction paper. He used 9 sheets for a science project. Express the amount of paper he used as both a decimal and a fraction.

_____

Short Response Question

22 Tyler has 100 baseball cards. He gave 7 cards to his friend. Tyler wrote the decimal 0.7 to represent the part of his collection he gave away. Did Tyler write the correct decimal? Explain your answer.

_____

_____

_____

Lesson 7.10 ▪ Predicting odd and even numbers

> **READY REFERENCE**
> **odd number** a number, such as 1, 3, and 5, that is not divisible by 2
> **even number** a number, such as 2, 4, and 6, that is divisible by 2

🗝 Think About It

Numbers can be classified as odd or even. Both odd and even numbers can be added, subtracted, and multiplied. Can you predict if the sum, difference, or product of two numbers will be odd or even?

🗝 Here's How

Adding odd and even numbers

1. If you add 2 even numbers, the sum is _____. $4 + 8 = 12$ $22 + 6 = 28$

2. If you add 2 odd numbers, the sum is _____. $3 + 9 = 12$ $11 + 7 = 18$

3. If you add an even number and an odd number, the sum is _____. $4 + 5 = 9$ $6 + 9 = 15$

Subtraction

1. If you subtract 2 even numbers, the difference is _____. $8 - 2 = 6$ $14 - 6 = 8$

2. If you subtract 2 odd numbers, the difference is _____. $13 - 3 = 10$ $19 - 7 = 12$

3. If you subtract an even number from an odd number, or an odd number from an even number, the difference is _____. $19 - 4 = 15$ $22 - 3 = 19$

Multiplication

1. If you multiply 2 even numbers, the product is _____. $6 \times 8 = 48$ $4 \times 2 = 8$

2. If you multiply 2 odd numbers, the product is _____. $5 \times 3 = 15$ $9 \times 3 = 27$

3. If you multiply an even and an odd number, the product is _____. $6 \times 3 = 18$ $9 \times 4 = 36$

 **Practice**

Predict whether the answer will be an odd number or an even number.

1 18 + 14 = _____

2 99 + 33 = _____

3 86 + 15 = _____

4 122 − 16 = _____

5 43 − 9 = _____

6 84 − 23 = _____

7 39 − 14 = _____

8 68 × 4 = _____

9 49 × 7 = _____

10 16 × 3 = _____

11 75 × 12 = _____

12 35 × 18 = _____

13 On Maple Avenue, odd-numbered addresses are on the left side of the street. Even-numbered addresses are on the right side of the street. Rico's house number is the product of 7 and 5. On what side of Maple Avenue does Rico live? Explain your answer.

_____

_____

14 Janet has two brothers. Tom is 9 years old and Dan is 5 years old. Janet's age is the sum of her brothers' ages. Is Janet's age an odd or an even number?

_____

Short Response Question

15 Kylie had $16. She spent $9 on a shirt. Is the amount of money left over an odd number or an even number? Her grandmother gave her $5 for her birthday. Does she now have an odd or even amount of money? Explain your answer and show your work.

_____

_____

Lesson 7.11 ▪ Area and volume with counting squares

> **READY REFERENCE**
> **area** the number of square units inside a plane figure
> **volume** the number of cubic units inside a space figure

🔑 Think About It

The figure shows the size of Dee's bedroom. Dee wants to buy a rug for the room. She knows what color and style she wants, but she doesn't know the size of the rug. Do you know how Dee can use the figure below to find the size of her bedroom?

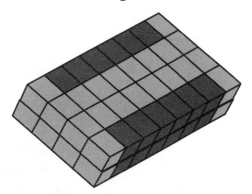

🔑 Here's How

Step 1 Find the area.

1. How many square units form the long side of the figure? _____

2. How many square units form the short side of the figure? _____

3. The area is the number of square units in the largest layer of the figure. Count the square units or use the formula length × width.

What is the area of the figure? _____ sq units

Step 2 Find the volume.

4. How many layers are in the figure? _____

5. How many cubes are in each layer? _____

6. The volume is the total number of cubes inside the figure. Count the cubes or solve by using the formula length × width × height.

What is the volume of the figure? _____

🗝 Practice

Find the area and volume by counting the cubes or using the formula.

1

Area _____ Volume _____

2

Volume _____

3

Volume _____

4

Area _____ Volume _____

5

Jeb used cubes to form a figure that represents his bedroom.

What is the area of the area of his bedroom? _____

What is the volume? _____

Short Response Question

6 If two figures have the same volume, do their bases have the same area? Explain why.

_____

_____

Lesson 7.12 ▪ Solve open sentences with missing information

> **READY REFERENCE**
> **open sentence** problem in which a number is missing and must be identified
> **table** list of facts in columns and rows

Think About It

There are 63 boxes of sneakers on three shelves in the storeroom of the Sneaker Shack. The top shelf holds the least number of boxes. The bottom shelf holds the greatest. Each shelf holds 7 more boxes than the shelf above it. There are 14 boxes of sneakers on the top shelf. Do you know how to determine the number of boxes on the other two shelves?

Here's How

Solve by writing an open sentence.

1. How many boxes are on the top shelf? _____
   What is the total number of boxes on all three shelves? _____

2. Can you solve this problem using addition? _____ Can you solve using subtraction? _____

3. Write an open sentence for addition or subtraction:

   $$\underset{14}{\underline{\text{Top shelf}}} \quad \underset{+\,(14+7)}{\underline{\text{Middle shelf}}} \quad \underset{+\,x\;=\;63}{\underline{\text{Bottom shelf}}}$$

   $$35 + x = 63$$
   $$x = \underline{}$$

Solve by making a table.

1. Use the information you know to complete the table.

Shelf	Number of Boxes
Top	14
Middle	_____
Bottom	_____

2. If each shelf holds 7 more boxes than the shelf above it, how many boxes are on the middle shelf? _____ On the bottom shelf? _____

3. How can you check your answer? _____

 **Practice**

Four boxes hold a total of 240 pencils. The boxes are placed in a line. The first box has the greatest number of pencils. The last box has the least number of pencils. Each box has twice as many pencils as the box behind it. The last box has 16 pencils. How many pencils are in all four boxes?

1 Use what you know to write an open sentence to show the total number of pencils in all four boxes.

_____

2 The problem states that each box has twice as many pencils as the box behind it. What does this tell you about the number of pencils in the third box?

_____

3 What do you know about the number of pencils in the second box?

_____

4 What do you know about the number of pencils in the first box?

_____

5 Make a table. Fill in the facts you know.

Box 1	Box 2	Box 3	Box 4

Short Response Question

6 A library bookcase with three shelves holds a total of 105 books. The top shelf has the least number of books. The bottom shelf has the greatest number of books. Each shelf holds 10 more books than the shelf above it. The middle shelf holds 35 books. How many books are on the top shelf? The bottom shelf? Show your work and explain how you solved the problem.

_____

_____

Lesson 7.13 ▪ Use open multiplication and division sentences in situations of equality and inequality

> **READY REFERENCE**
> < less than
> > greater than

 Think About It

Tami saved $5 to buy stickers. At Sticker World, 4 packs of 8 stickers each cost $5. At Toy Stop and Shop, 5 packs of 6 stickers each cost $5. How can Tami figure out where she will get the most stickers for her money?

 Here's How

Use open multiplication sentences.

Step 1 Write multiplication facts.

Sticker World	**Toy Stop and Shop**
Number of packs = _____	Number of packs = _____
Stickers in each pack = _____	Stickers in each pack = _____
Multiplication fact: $4 \times 8 = n$	Multiplication fact: _____

Step 2 Compare the amounts.

1. Write each multiplication fact.

   $4 \times$ _____   _____ $\times 6$

2. Find the products. Write them on the lines. _____ ? _____

3. Compare the amounts. Replace the ? with <, >, or =.

   _____ _____ _____

4. Where should Tami buy her stickers? _____

🔑 Practice

Al can buy 2 packages of juice that each hold 4 juice boxes or 3 packages of juice that each hold 3 juice boxes for the same amount of money.

1 What multiplication facts show the number of juice boxes in each pack?

_____ and _____

2 Find the products. _____ and _____

3 Compare the products. Use <, >, or =. _____ _____ _____

4 What should Al buy to get the most juice for his money? _____

Compare the amounts. Write <, >, or = on the line.

5 8×5 ____ 4×10 **6** 3×9 ____ 5×5 **7** $28 \div 4$ ____ $18 \div 3$

8 6×4 ____ 8×3 **9** 8×8 ____ 10×7 **10** $100 \div 10$ ____ 5×2

11 Mrs. Ling can buy 2 packs of hot dogs that each have 10 hot dogs. Or, she can buy 3 packs of hot dogs that each have 6 hot dogs for the same amount of money.

Which is the better buy? _____ Show your work.

Short Response Question

12 Tim is 10 and Wendy is 9. Tim says that he can write two different number sentences that describe their age differences. Write the number sentences. Explain how you solved the problem.

_____

_____

_____

Lesson 7.14 ▪ Use formulas to find perimeter and area

> **READY REFERENCE**
> **perimeter** the distance around a figure
> **area** the number of square units needed to cover a flat surface

 Think About It

Sashi made a rectangular flower garden. It is 4 feet long and 3 feet wide. Sashi wants to put a fence around the edge of the garden. She also wants to put some plastic over the garden. Do you know how Sashi can find the amount of fencing and plastic she needs?

 Here's How

Step 1 Find the perimeter.

1. Perimeter is the distance around a figure. The formula for perimeter of a rectangle is *Perimeter = (2 × length) + (2 × width)*. Write the number sentence you will use to find the perimeter of the garden.

_____

2. Solve the number sentence. How much fencing does Sashi need?

_____

Step 2 Find the area.

3. Area is the space inside a figure. The formula for area of a rectangle is *Area = length × width*. Write the number sentence you will use to find the area of the garden.

_____

4. Solve the number sentence. How much plastic does Sashi need?

_____

 Practice

Bill's bedroom is 9 feet long and 7 feet wide. He wants to put a wallpaper border along all four walls of his room. He also wants to put in new wall-to-wall carpeting.

1 What is the shape of Bill's bedroom? _____

2 Should Bill find the perimeter or the area to determine the amount of border he needs?

_____

3 Write the number sentence Bill can use to find the amount of border needed.

_____ Solve the sentence. _____

4 Should Bill find perimeter or area to determine the rug size needed? _____

5 Write the number sentence Bill can use to find the amount of rug needed.

_____ Solve the sentence. _____

Find the perimeter and area for each figure.

6 perimeter _____

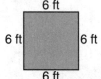

6 ft
6 ft   6 ft
6 ft

7 area _____

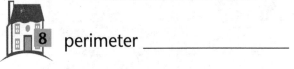

8 perimeter _____

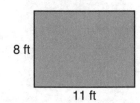

8 ft

9 area _____

11 ft

10 The Wilson family is planting a vegetable garden.
The length of the garden is double the width.
The garden is 4 feet wide. What is the shape of the garden? _____
What formula would you use to find its perimeter? _____
What is the perimeter? _____

Short Response Question

11 Zeke read that a square room was 12 feet wide. Can Zeke find the perimeter and area of this room with this one measurement? Show your work and explain your answer.

_____

_____

Lesson 7.15 ▪ Use counters to solve division problems

> **READY REFERENCE**
> **dividend** the number to be divided
> **divisor** the number by which another number is divided
> **quotient** the answer in division

 **Think About It**

Trudy baked 18 muffins. She wants to divide them evenly among 3 containers. How can you use counters to find how many muffins Trudy should put in each container?

❖  **Here's How**

Step 1 Use a model for the dividend.

1. How many muffins does Trudy have altogether? _____
   Place this number of counters on a flat surface.

Step 2 Name the divisor.

2. How many containers will the muffins be placed into? _____
   What is the divisor? _____

Step 3 Use the dividend and divisor to find the quotient.

3. Separate the counters into 3 equal groups.
   How many counters are in one group? _____
   What is the quotient? _____
   How many muffins will be in each container? _____

4. Write the division fact that you modeled with the counters.

   _____

❖ **Practice**

Use counters to solve the problems.

1 $12 \div 2 =$ _____

2 $21 \div 7 =$ _____

3 $25 \div$ _____ $= 5$

4 $16 \div$ _____ $= 4$

5 18 ÷ 2 = _____

6 35 ÷ 5 = _____

7 42 ÷ _____ = 7

8 32 ÷ _____ = 4

9 30 ÷ 5 = _____

10 56 ÷ 8 = _____

11 Will baked 48 cupcakes. He wants to store the cupcakes in containers of six. How many containers does he need? _____

12 Manuel, Bob, and Louis earned $36 washing cars. How can they divide the money equally? _____

13 Tara and Vicki picked berries all day. They need to divide the 30 quarts of berries into baskets. Each basket holds 5 quarts of berries. How many baskets do they need? _____

Short Response Question

14 Nine students are going on a picnic. They have 15 juice boxes. Are there enough juice boxes for each person to drink two? Explain your answer and show your work.

_____

_____

_____

Lesson 7.16 ▪ Use counters to explore square numbers and triangular numbers

> **READY REFERENCE**
> **square number** the product of a number multiplied by itself

 Think About It

On Monday, Joel wrote 2 pages of a report. On Tuesday, he wrote twice as many pages. On Wednesday, Joel again wrote twice as many pages. How many pages did Joel write on Tuesday and Wednesday? How can you use counters to answer this question?

  Here's How

Find square numbers.

Step 1 Model the items.

1. Place 2 counters on your desk to represent the number of pages written on Monday. If Joel wrote twice as many pages on Tuesday, you need to place 2 more counters. How many pages has he written so far?
$2 \times 2 = $ _____

Step 2 Find and extend the pattern.

2. Joel has now written 4 pages. On Wednesday he wrote twice as many pages. Use your counters to show the problem:
$4 \times$ _____ $=$ _____

3. Compare the counters that represent Tuesday with those that represent Wednesday. How did they change?

_____

4. You used counters to show a square number. You can draw arrays too.

   4 squared $= 4 \times 4 = $ _____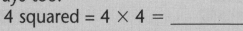

5. Can you extend the pattern to Thursday?_____
Draw an array and write the problem.

Find triangular numbers.

Look at these triangular numbers. Can you complete the pattern for the triangular number 10?

1   3   6   10

 Practice

Use counters or draw arrays to solve the problems.

1 Mr. O'Hara sold 8 televisions on Monday. On Wednesday he sold 8 squared. How many televisions did he sell on Wednesday? _____

2 Caroline started her collection with 3 butterflies. If she squares the number of butterflies for 2 days, how many butterflies will she have? _____

Complete the pattern and tell whether the number is a squared number or a triangular number.

3 4, 16, _____, _____

4 10, 15, 21, _____

_____   _____

Short Response Question

5 Study the triangular number patterns in the first box. Explain how you can use the pattern to determine the triangular number in the second box. Write the numbers next to the triangular number to prove your explanation.

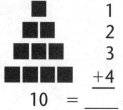

1
2
+3
6 = ___

1
2
3
+4
10 = ___

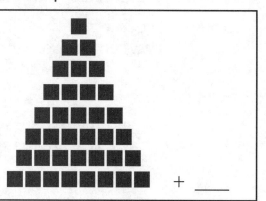

+ ___

Lesson 7.17 ▪ Use counters with open sentences

> **READY REFERENCE**
>
> **open sentence** problem in which a number is missing and must be identified

◆ 🔑 Think About It

Dylan and Pete went fishing yesterday. Together, they caught 26 fish. Dylan caught 13 fish. Do you know how to use counters to find the number of fish Pete caught?

🔑 Here's How

Step 1 Write an open sentence.

1. What do you need to find? _____ What do you know? _____

2. How many fish did Dylan catch? _____ How many fish did the boys catch altogether? _____

3. Circle the open sentence you can use to solve the problem.

   $13 - \square = 26$ $26 + \square = 13$ $13 + \square = 26$

Step 2 Model one addend.

4. How many fish did Dylan catch? _____ Put his number of counters in a pile.

Step 3 Add on.

5. How many fish did the boys catch altogether? _____ Make another pile of counters that models Pete's fish. Begin counting at 14. Stop counting at 26. How many fish did Pete catch? _____

6. Complete the open sentence you circled in number 3.

   _____

Practice

Use counters to solve the problems.

1 17 + _____ = 26

2 _____ − 8 = 13

3 20 − _____ = 7

4 _____ + 12 = 23

5 _____ + 15 = 31

6 17 + _____ = 24

7 _____ − 11 = 14

8 39 − _____ = 13

9 40 − _____ = 15

10 _____ + 22 = 37

 11 During the past two months, Julie has read a total of 28 books. Last month, she read 13 books. How many books did Julie read this month? Write an open sentence and solve.

_____

Short Response Question

12 Mike just bought 32 baseball cards. Of these cards, 7 are doubles—cards he already owns. Explain how you can use counters to find the number of new cards that are not doubles.

_____

_____

_____

Lesson 7.18 ▪ Use counters to explore commutative and associative properties

🔑 Think About It

Rose and Zack need to find the sum of 18 and 14. Rose wrote 18 + 14 = ?
Zack wrote 14 + 18 = ? Do you know how to use counters to see if they will
get the same sum?

🔑 Here's How

Step 1 Solve the first equation.

1. What is the first addend in Rose's equation? _____ Put this amount of counters in a pile.

2. What is the second addend in Rose's equation? _____ Add this number of counters to the pile.

3. What is the total number of counters in the pile? _____

Step 2 Solve the second equation.

4. What is the first addend in Zack's equation? _____ Put this amount of counters in a pile.

5. What is the second addend in Zack's equation? _____ Add this amount of counters to the pile.

6. What is the total number of counters in the pile? _____

Step 3 Compare the sums.

7. Are the sums the same or different? _____

8. What does this tell you about the order of adding numbers?

_____

Practice

Use counters to solve the problems.

1 22 + _____ = 16 + 22

2 _____ + 8 = 8 + 17

3 10 + _____ = 8 + 10

4 _____ + 31 = 31 + 15

5 _____ × 4 = 4 × 11

6 9 × _____ = 8 × 9

7 5 × 7 = 7 × _____

8 _____ × 3 = 3 × 6

9 5 + _____ + 6) = (5 + 8) + 6

10 (3 + 9) + 12 = 3 + _____ + 12)

11 _____ + (6 + 15) = (2 + 6) + 15

12 (7 + 4) + _____ = 7 + (4 + 5)

 13 Rhea needs to find the product of 7 and 8. Write two multiplication sentences she can use to find this product.

_____

_____

Short Response Question

14 Jill read 6 pages of a book on Monday. On Tuesday she read 5 pages in the morning and 3 pages in the evening. On Monday Tiko read 6 pages in the morning and 5 pages in the evening. On Tuesday Tiko read 3 pages. Who read more pages? Write a problem to show how many pages Jill read. Write a problem to show how many pages Tiko read. How are the problems alike and different?

_____

_____

_____

Lesson 7.19 ▪ Tangrams and pattern blocks

Think About It

Rico has the tangram pieces shown below. He must put the puzzle pieces together to form Shape A. Do you know what he should do to solve this problem?

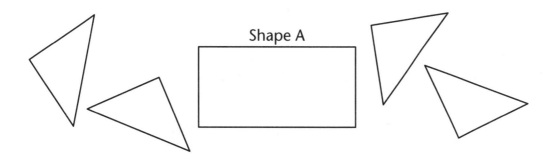

Shape A

Here's How

Step 1 Describe the tangram pieces.

    1. What is the shape of Rico's tangram pieces? _____

    2. Suppose Rico has 2 of the tangram pieces. If he places the long sides next to each other and touching, what shape would result?

    _____

Step 2 Describe shape A.

    3. What is the shape Rico needs to form? _____

    4. Form a second square with the remaining two pieces.

    5. Place the two squares next to each other to form shape A.

Practice

Use the shapes below to answer Problems 1–5.

Mae's Pattern Block   Shape B

Mae has a pattern block. She wants to use copies of her pattern block to form shape B.

1 What is the shape of Mae's pattern block? _____

2 What is the shape Mae wants to form? _____

3 Suppose Mae arranges two of her pattern blocks so that they meet along the long side. What shape results? _____

4 How many squares this size are in the shape Mae wants to form? _____

5 How many pattern blocks does Mae need to form shape B? _____

Look at the shapes below to answer Problem 6.

6 Look at the pattern block below labeled Shape A. What is its shape? _____ How many Shape A pattern blocks can you find in Shape B? _____ Now look at Shape C. How many Shape C pattern blocks can you find in Shape B? _____

Shape A

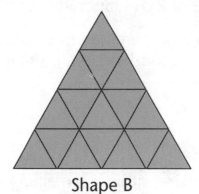

Shape B

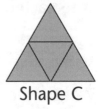

Shape C

Short Response Question

7 Sketch a shape that can be formed from six copies of Mae's pattern blocks. Explain how you decided on the shape to sketch.

_____

_____

_____

Lesson 7.20 ▪ Use manipulatives or calculators to skip count and multiply

◆ ▣ Think About It

Sasha has six bags of counters. Each bag contains 5 counters. Do you know what multiplication fact Sasha can use to find the total number of counters in the bags?

▣ Here's How

Step 1 Model the problem.

1. How many bags are there? _____

2. How many counters are in each bag? _____

3. Arrange your counters into 6 groups with 5 counters in each group.

Step 2 Use skip counting.

4. How many counters are in each group?_____

Skip count by 5 to find the total. 5, _____

How many counters are there altogether? _____

Step 3 Name the multiplication fact.

5. One of the factors is the number of groups you have.

What is this factor? _____

The other factor is the number of counters in each group.

What is this factor? _____

The product is the total number of counters.

What is the product? _____

6. Write the multiplication fact. _____

Practice

1 Tony has 4 packs of gum. There are 4 sticks of gum in each pack. If Tony wants to skip count to find the total number of sticks, what numbers will he say?

_____

What multiplication fact can Tony use to find this total? _____

2 Dixie bought 7 packs of erasers. There are 3 erasers in each pack. If Dixie wants to skip count to find the total number of erasers, what numbers will she say?

_____

What multiplication fact can Dixie use to find this total? _____

3 Tia bought 5 packs of stickers. There are 8 stickers in each pack. If Tia wants to skip count to find the total number of stickers, what numbers will she say?

_____

What multiplication fact can Tia use to find this total? _____

4 Mrs. Ruiz bought 6 bags of potatoes. Each bag holds 5 pounds. How can she skip count to find the total number of pounds of potatoes?

_____

Short Response Question

5 Van needs 24 pounds of apples. The market sells 2 lb bags of apples and 6 lb boxes of apples. How can Van use skip counting to find the number of bags or boxes he should buy?

Part A 2 lb bags _____

_____

multiplication fact _____

Part B 6 lb bags _____

_____

multiplication fact _____

Lesson 7.21 ▪ Use manipulative materials to explore symmetry

> **READY REFERENCE**
> **line of symmetry** a line that divides a shape into two halves that are exactly alike

🔑 Think About It

Carl wants to know if the dotted line in the figure is a line of symmetry. He copied the figure onto a sheet of paper. Do you know how Carl can use the paper to determine if the line is a line of symmetry?

🔑 Here's How

Step 1 Make a model.

1. Place a sheet of paper over the figure. Trace the figure and the dotted line.

2. Carefully fold the paper along the dotted line. Do the outlines of the two halves overlap one another exactly? _____

Step 2 Classify the dotted line.

3. Open the paper. Carefully observe the two halves. Are they exactly alike? _____

4. Is the dotted line a line of symmetry? _____

🔑 Practice

Create a model of each figure. Write yes or no to tell whether the dotted line is a line of symmetry.

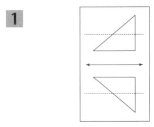

_____

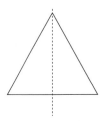

_____

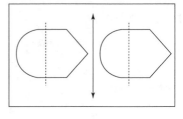

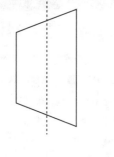

_____

_____

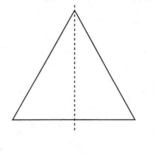

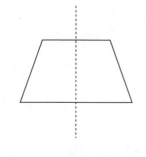

_____

_____

Short Response Question

7 Look at the figures. Draw a line of symmetry on each one if possible. Can you draw a line of symmetry on the horse and the house? Explain your answers.

_____

_____

_____

_____

Lesson 7.22 ▪ Use manipulative materials to explore linear patterns

> **READY REFERENCE**
> **pattern** a series of items or actions that appear to happen in a specific order

Think About It

Look at the pattern below. Each figure is made with paper clips. Do you know how to determine the number of paper clips needed to make the next figure in the pattern?

Figure 1

Figure 2

Figure 3

Here's How

Step 1 Compare the items.

1. How many clips make up the first figure? _____

2. How are they arranged? _____

3. How many clips make up the second figure? _____

4. How are they arranged? _____

5. How many clips make up the third figure? _____

6. How are they arranged? _____

Step 2 Describe the pattern.

7. What pattern is used to create the figures?

_____

Step 3 Use manipulatives.

8. If this pattern continues, how many clips will make up the fourth figure? _____

9. Use paper clips to form the fourth figure. What does it look like?

_____

Practice

Use paper clips to complete the pattern. Then answer the questions about the figures you made.

Figure 1   Figure 2   Figure 3

1 What pattern is used to make the figures?

_____

2 How many clips are needed to make the next figure in this pattern? _____

3 Sketch the next figure in the pattern.

Figure 1   Figure 2   Figure 3

4 How many clips are needed to make the next figure in this pattern? _____

5 Sketch the next figure in the pattern.

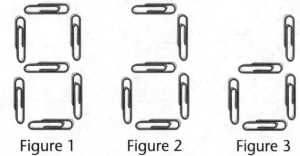

Figure 1   Figure 2   Figure 3

 6 How many clips are needed to make the next figure in this pattern? _____

7 Sketch the next figure in the pattern.

Short Response Question

8 Create a paper clip pattern. Use 3 clips in your first figure, 5 clips in your second figure, and 7 clips in your third figure. Draw your pattern and explain how you created your pattern.

_____

Lesson 7.23 ▪ Find the mode, median, mean, and range of a set of data

> **READY REFERENCE**
> **range** in a set of data, the difference between the greatest number and the least number
> **mean** in a set of data, the sum of the numbers divided by the total number of numbers
> **median** the middle number in a set of data
> **mode** in a set of data, the numeral that occurs most often

Think About It

Ten students were asked how many hours they spend each week working on homework. Their answers are shown in the bar graph. Their answers are: 5, 6, 7, 8, 3, 5, and 6. How do you find the range, median, mean, and mode of this data?

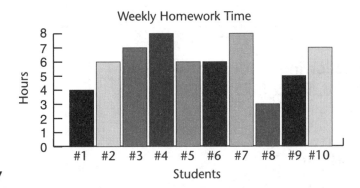

Here's How

Step 1 Find the range.

1. What is the highest number in the data? _____

What is the lowest number? _____
The range is the difference between these numbers.

What is the range? _____

Step 2 Find the mean.

2. How many bars are there? _____

What is the sum of the values of the bars? _____
Divide the sum by the number of bars. The quotient is the mean.

What is the mean? _____

Step 3 Find the median.

3. Write the value of each bar in order from least to greatest.

_____

4. What is the middle number? _____

Step 4 Find the mode.

5. The bar that appears most often is the mode. Look at the bars.

What is the mode? _____

Practice

Find the range, mean, median, and mode of each set of data. Write your answers on the lines.

1 Data: 3, 8, 3, 1, 5, 3, 7, 3, 3

Range _____   Mean _____   Median _____   Mode _____

2 Data: 14, 12, 11, 9, 18, 12, 13, 12, 8, 11

Range _____   Mean _____   Median _____   Mode _____

3 Julie received the following grades on five math quizzes: 88, 92, 90, 95, and 85. What is the mean of her scores?   _____

Short Response Question

4 Six adults were asked how many hours they spend each week talking on the telephone. Here are their responses: 12, 18, 9, 13, 14, and 12. Explain how to find the range, mean, median, and mode of this data.

_____

_____

_____

_____

_____

_____

Lesson 7.24 ▪ Compare frequencies in bar graphs or histograms

> **READY REFERENCE**
> **bar graph** a graph that uses bars of different heights to show data
> **histogram** a bar graph that shows the number of times data occur
> **frequency** how often an event occurs

🔑 Think About It

Sal asked five classmates how much time they spend playing video games each week. He showed the results in a bar graph. Do you know how to find the frequencies of responses?

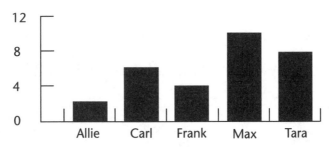

🔑 Here's How

Step 1 Read the labels.

    1. What does the vertical axis show? _____

    2. How is it labeled? _____

    3. What does the horizontal axis show? _____

    4. How is it labeled? _____

Step 2 Identify the responses.

    5. Look at the height of each bar to write each student's response.

      Allie _____   Carl _____   Frank _____

      Max _____   Tara _____

Step 3 Find the frequencies.

    6. How many times was a response between 0 and 4 hours? _____

    7. How many times was a response between 5 and 8 hours? _____

    8. How many times was a response between 9 and 12 hours? _____

    9. Which of these had the greatest frequency? _____

Practice

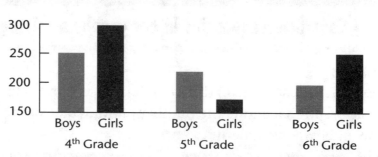

1 How should the vertical axis be labeled? _____

2 How should the horizontal axis be labeled? _____

3 Why are the bars in the graph shaded differently?

_____

4 Complete the table to show the number of cans collected by each group.

Group	Number of Cans
4th Grade Boys	
4th Grade Girls	
5th Grade Boys	
5th Grade Girls	
6th Grade Boys	
6th Grade Girls	

5 Suppose you needed to make a histogram of this data. Write the frequency of each set of data.

Set of Data	Frequency
Between 150 and 200 cans	
Between 201 and 250 cans	
Between 251 and 300 cans	

Short Response Question

6 How are a bar graph and a histogram alike and different? Make a frequency histogram of the data from problem 5.

_____

_____

Lesson 7.25 ▪ Describe trends in bar graphs and line graphs

🔑 Think About It

The snack bar at TriTown Cinema is very busy on Saturdays. The manager wants to hire another worker. She made a graph to show the number of customers who visited the snack bar during a 10-hour period last Saturday. Do you know how to read the graph to determine during which 3-hour period the new worker should be scheduled?

🔑 Here's How

Step 1 Read the axes.

1. What does the vertical axis show? _____

2. What does the horizontal axis show? _____

Step 2 Read the graph.

3. Look at the height of each line to identify the number of people in the store for each time. For example, from noon to 1:00, there were _____ people.

Step 3 Look for trends in the data.

4. How does the data change between noon and 3:00?

_____

5. How does the data change between 3:00 and 6:00?

_____

Step 4 Use the information.

6. When did the greatest number of customers visit the snack bar?

_____

7. When should the new worker be scheduled? _____

Practice

Look at the graph, and answer the questions.

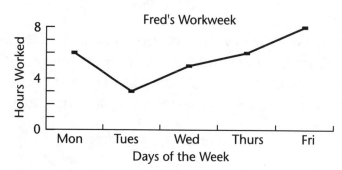

Fred's Workweek

1 What does the graph show? _____

2 Complete the table to show the number of hours Fred worked each day.

	Mon	**Tues**	**Wed**	**Thurs**	**Fri**
Hours					

3 How does the number of hours Fred worked change between Monday and Wednesday? _____

4 How does the number of hours Fred worked change between Wednesday and Friday? _____

5 Based on the trend shown in the graph, do you think Fred would work more than 4 hours or less than 4 hours on Saturday? Give reasons for your answer.

_____

_____

Short Response Question

6 A prediction is a statement about a future event based on known information. How can finding trends in a graph help you make a prediction?

_____

_____

_____

Lesson 7.26 ▪ Prisms, pyramids, cones, and cylinders

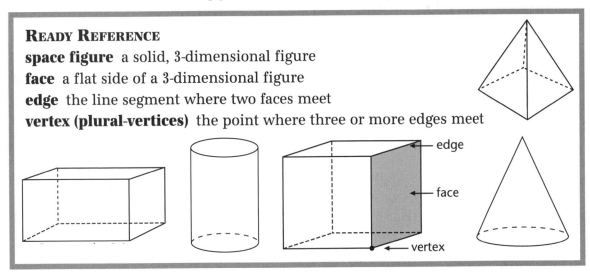

READY REFERENCE

space figure a solid, 3-dimensional figure

face a flat side of a 3-dimensional figure

edge the line segment where two faces meet

vertex (plural-vertices) the point where three or more edges meet

 Think About It

Zoe is making models of a pyramid, a rectangular prism, a cone, and a cylinder. She will cut flat shapes from cardboard and glue them together to form her models. For example, Zoe can see she will need triangles to form the shape of the square pyramid. Study the geometric shapes above. Then complete the table below.

 Here's How

Look at the figures above. For each figure, write how many edges, vertices, and faces there are. Then write the shapes of the faces in each figure.

Name	Edges	Vertices	Faces	Shapes of Faces
Rectangular Prism				
Square Pyramid				
Cone				
Cylinder				

🔑 Practice

Name the space figures in Problems 1–3.

1

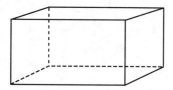

_____

2

_____

3

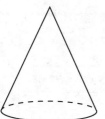

_____

4

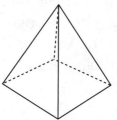

_____

 5 Name three items in your home that are cylinders. _____

_____

Short Response Question

6 How are the space figures in this lesson alike? How are they different?

_____

_____

Lesson 7.27 ▪ Identify different types of prisms and pyramids

> **READY REFERENCE**
> **prism** a 3-dimensional shape with a similar top and bottom
> **square pyramid** a 3-dimensional shape with a flat bottom and pointed top

 Think About It

Jim made two models. He must classify each one. Do you know how Jim should classify his 3-dimensional figures?

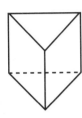

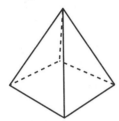

Model A   Model B

 Here's How

Step 1 Name the traits of each model.

1. Describe the top and bottom of Model A.

   _____

2. What 2-dimensional shapes form the faces of Model A?

   _____

3. Describe the top and bottom of Model B.

   _____

4. What 2-dimensional shapes form the faces of Model B?

   _____

Step 2 Classify the models.

5. Is Model A a prism or a pyramid? _____

6. Is Model B a prism or a pyramid? _____

Practice

Circle the name of each 3-dimensional figure.

1

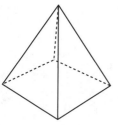

triangular prism

rectangular prism

2

square pyramid

rectangular prism

3

square pyramid

triangular prism

 4 Name three items in your home that are prisms. Tell what kind of prism they are.

_____

_____

Short Response Question

5 How are a triangular prism and a rectangular prism alike? How do they differ?

_____

_____

_____

Lesson 7.28 • Find two-and three-dimensional shapes in nature, art, and the environment

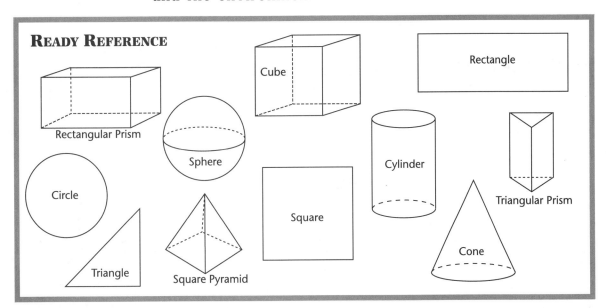

READY REFERENCE

Rectangular Prism

Cube

Rectangle

Sphere

Cylinder

Triangular Prism

Circle

Square

Triangle

Square Pyramid

Cone

🔑 Think About It

Sam is working on a math project. He must classify objects in his home according to their shapes. Do you know how Sam can classify objects?

🔑 Here's How

Recognize the traits of two-dimensional figures.

1. A two-dimensional figure is a closed, flat figure. Which figures above are two-dimensional figures? _____

_____

Recognize the traits of three-dimensional figures.

1. Which figures above are three-dimensional figures?

_____

2. All the faces of a _____ are squares.

3. A _____ has 3 rectangular faces and 2 triangles.

4. All the faces of a _____ are rectangles.

5. Two faces of a _____ are circles. The third face is a rectangle.

🔑 Practice

Classify the objects.

1 a slice of pie _____

2 a slice of a tree trunk _____

3 a shoe box _____

Classify the figures.

1

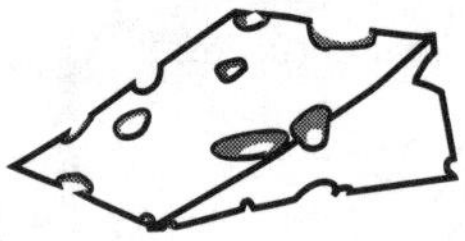

_____

2

_____

3

_____

4

_____

5

_____

6

_____

7 Name three items in your home that are rectangular prisms.

_____

Short Response Question

8 How are a triangle and a square pyramid related?

_____

_____

_____

Lesson 7.29 • Find examples of tessellations in the real world

> **READY REFERENCE**
>
> **tessellation** a pattern of shapes that completely cover an area without overlapping or leaving gaps

 ## Think About It

Mitchell was asked to name a tessellation that occurs in nature. He carefully observed a section of a honeycomb and a pine cone. Do you know how to determine if they are tessellations?

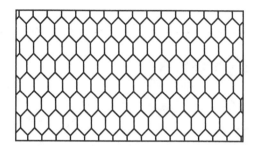 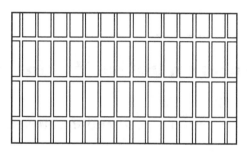

 ## Here's How

Step 1 Recognize the traits of tessellations.

    1. How do you know when a pattern is a tessellation? It does not _____ or leave any _____

Step 2 Observe the traits of the honeycomb.

    2. What shape makes up the honeycomb? _____

    3. Are there spaces between the shapes? _____ Do any of the shapes overlap? _____

    4. Is the honeycomb a tessellation? _____

Step 3 Observe the traits of a pine cone.

    5. What shape makes up the pine cone? _____

    6. Are there spaces between the shapes? _____ Do any of the shapes overlap? _____

    7. Is the pine cone a tessellation? _____

 **Practice**

Jed painted this pattern as a border around his room.

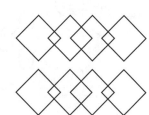

1 What shape makes up the pattern? _____

2 Are there spaces between the shapes? _____

Do the shapes overlap? _____

3 Is Jed's pattern a tessellation? _____ Why? _____

_____

Mrs. Wilkes covered her kitchen floor with this pattern of tiles.

4 What shape makes up the pattern? _____

5 Are there spaces between the shapes? _____

Do the shapes overlap? _____

6 Is the floor pattern a tessellation? _____ Why? _____

_____

Short Response Question

7 Create your own tessellation. Sketch your pattern in the space below. Then explain how you formed the pattern.

_____

_____

_____

Lesson 7.30 • Identify examples of symmetry in nature, art, and music

> **READY REFERENCE**
> **line of symmetry** a line that divides a shape into two halves that are exactly alike

 Think About It

Rhea observed this flower. She thinks that it has more than one line of symmetry. Do you know how Rhea can find all the lines of symmetry in the flower?

 Here's How

Step 1 Make a model.

1. Trace the flower or draw a sketch on a sheet of paper. Be sure that your sketch shows the same number of petals as the flower. Be sure that the petals are in the same location as the flower.

Step 2 Use the model.

2. Fold the paper in half. Do the halves match? _____ If so, the fold is a line of symmetry.

3. Try folding the paper in half in a different way. Do the halves match? _____ If so, the fold is a second line of symmetry.

4. Continue folding the paper in new ways. Check to see if each new fold is a line of symmetry.

5. How many times did you fold your paper? _____

   How many lines of symmetry did you find? _____

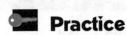 Practice

Trace or create a model of each figure. Use your model to find all the lines of symmetry. Then draw a line on the figures below to show each line of symmetry.

1

2

3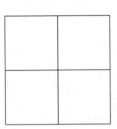

4

Write yes or no under each shape to tell if the dashed line is a line of symmetry.

5

_____   _____   _____   _____   _____   _____

Short Response Question

6 Draw a figure that has no lines of symmetry. Explain why your drawing has no lines of symmetry.

_____

_____

_____

Lesson 7.31 • Relate the concept of fraction to the value of notes in music

🔑 Think About It

Jon is taking a music class. He learned that a whole note equals 4 quarter notes. He also learned that a whole note equals 2 half notes.

🔑 Here's How

Step 1 Make a chart.

   1. Organize what Jon knows in a chart.

Type of Note	Part of a Whole Note
Whole	1
Half	
Quarter	

Step 2 Look for relationships.

   2. How many halves make up one whole? _____

   3. How many half notes make up one whole note? _____

   4. How many fourths make up one whole? _____

   5. How many quarter notes make up one whole note? _____

Step 3 Use the information to draw conclusions.

   6. How many quarter notes equal one whole note? _____

   7. Write the whole number or fraction next to each note.

   Whole note _____   Half note _____   Quarter note _____

🔑 Practice

Circle the answer to each question.

1 How many quarter notes equal one half note?

One   Two   Four

2 How many half notes equal two whole notes?

Two   Four   Eight

3 How many quarter notes equal two whole notes?

One   Four   Eight

4 Jon played 6 half notes. How many whole notes is this equal to?

One   Two   Three

5 Jon played 12 quarter notes. How many whole notes is this equal to?

Two   Three   Four

6 Another musician played 8 half notes. How many quarter notes is this equal to?

Four   Eight   Sixteen

7 The musician played 4 whole notes. How many half notes is this equal to?

Eight   Sixteen   Twenty

8 Jon played one whole note and one half note. How many quarter notes is this
equal to? _____

Short Response Question

9 Alice wrote the fraction $\frac{1}{4}$ to represent the note she played. What type of note was
it? Explain your reasoning.

_____

_____

_____

Lesson 7.32 ▪ Relate examples of children's literature to mathematics

🔑 Think About It

A fairy tale describes a young woman who can turn straw into gold. On the first day, she turned one bag of straw into two bags of gold. On the second day, she turned two bags of straw into four bags of gold. On the third day, she turned four bags of straw into eight bags of gold. She continued this pattern for five days. Do you know how to find how many bags of gold she made on the fifth day?

🔑 Here's How

Step 1 Make a chart.

1. Organize what you know.

Day	Bags of Straw	Bags of Gold
1		
2		
3		
4		
5		

Step 2 Continue the pattern.

2. How many bags of straw did she have on the fourth day? _____

3. How many bags of gold did she make on the fourth day? _____

4. How many bags of straw did she have on the fifth day? _____

5. How many bags of gold did she make on the fifth day? _____

Step 3 Describe the pattern.

6. What pattern did you find?

_____

_____

_____

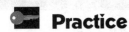 **Practice**

A very wealthy king decided to share some of his money with the local townspeople. He set aside $1,000. Each day, he gave away half of his money. Draw a chart to show your work.

1 How much money did the king give away on the fourth day?

2 Will the king run out of money? _____ Why or why not? _____

_____

Extended Response Question

3 Another folk tale tells the story of a spell that was cast a spell on a newborn baby boy. The spell caused the boy to age 5 years for each year that passed. Show your work in a chart.

Part A How old was the boy 3 years after the day of his birth? _____

Part B How old was the boy 6 years after the day of his birth? _____

Part C How many years after the day of his birth did the boy turn 50? _____

Part D Explain how you found the answers.

_____

_____

_____

_____

Directions
Use a separate piece of paper to show your work.

1 What is the next number in the pattern? 2, 5, 9, 14, ____

  A 16   **C** 20
  B 19   **D** 26

2 Which number sentence can be used to find 4×5?

  F $4 + 4 + 5 + 5$ **H** $4 + 4 + 4 + 4$
  G $5 + 5 + 5 + 5$ **J** $4 + 5$

3 Russ read $\frac{7}{10}$ of a book. What decimal shows the part of the book Russ read?

  A 0.70   **C** 0.07
  B 0.007   **D** 0.707

4 Bud made a flower garden in this shape. What is the perimeter of his garden?

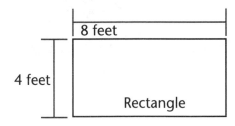

8 feet

4 feet

Rectangle

  F 12 feet   **H** 20 feet
  G 16 feet   **J** 24 feet

5 Beth has 28 muffins. She wants to divide them equally among 7 friends. How many muffins will each friend receive?

  A 3   **C** 6
  B 4   **D** 8

6 How many lines of symmetry does the figure have?

  F 2   **H** 4
  G 3   **J** 5

7 Jon received a homework pass after reading 25 pages of his book. On what day did he receive the pass?

Mon Tues Wed Thurs Fri

  A Tuesday   **C** Thursday
  B Wednesday   **D** Friday

8 What 2-dimensional figure forms the faces of this cube?

  F rectangle   **H** circle
  G triangle   **J** square

9 How many lines of symmetry does this figure have?

  A 1   **C** 4
  B 2   **D** 6

MULTIPLE CHOICE QUESTIONS

You are given several answer choices for multiple choice questions. You need to choose the correct answer from the choices you are given. There are some easy things you can do to help you with multiple choice questions.

1. Read the problem or question carefully.
2. Look at the answers and eliminate any that you know are wrong.
3. Solve the problem.
4. Check your work.
5. Choose the answer that matches your solution.

SHORT RESPONSE AND EXTENDED RESPONSE QUESTIONS

Short Response Questions ask you to do more than just solve a problem. You may be asked to show how you solved the problem and explain your answer.

Extended Response Questions are like Short Response Questions except they are longer and may take more than one step. Extended Response Questions take longer to complete, so be patient and take the time you need. Here are some tips for answering Short and Extended Response Questions.

1. Read the question carefully. Think about what you are asked to write.
2. Decide what you must do to solve the problem.
3. Solve the problem.
4. Check your answer.
5. Explain how you solved the problem.
6. When you have finished writing, look back at the question and make sure you have answered all the parts.

More Tips!

Sometimes answering a question means you will have to draw a picture, show an answer, or write or explain how you got the answer. Make sure you know exactly what you are supposed to do by reading the directions carefully. Reading the question more than once is helpful. If you do not understand the directions, ask your teacher to explain them.

 means use your ruler.

 means use your pattern blocks.

 means use your counters.

A

addition finding the sum of two or more numbers

angle two rays with the same endpoint

area the number of square units needed to cover a flat surface

array objects in rows and columns

associative property more than two numbers can be added in groups of two in any order and more than two numbers can be multiplied in groups of two in any order

associative property of addition changing the grouping of the addends does not change the sum

associative property of multiplication changing the grouping of the factors does not change the product

B

bar graph a graph that uses bars of different heights to show data

C

capacity the amount of liquid a container can hold

chord a line segment with both of its endpoints on a circle

circumference distance around a circle

clustering estimating by using numbers that are close to a rounded number

commutative property two or more numbers can be added in any order and two numbers can be multiplied in any order

commutative property of addition changing the order of the addends does not change the sum

commutative property of multiplication changing the order of the factors does not change the product

compare to examine two or more numbers to see which is greater or lesser

comparisons examinations of objects to see how they are alike so a measurement can be estimated

compatible numbers numbers that are easily computed mentally; two numbers—one of which divides the other evenly

compensation a mental math strategy in which finding a sum, difference, product, or quotient is made easier by using simpler numbers, such as tens or hundreds

composite number a whole number greater than 1 with more than two factors

D

data gathered facts or information

decimal a number with one or more places to the right of the decimal point

denominator names the total number of equal parts; the number under the fraction bar

diameter a line segment that passes through the center of a circle and has both endpoints on the circle

difference the answer in subtraction

digit a symbol used to write whole numbers (0, 1, 2, 3, 4, 5, 6, 7, 8, and 9)

distributive property to multiply a sum or difference by a number, multiply each number of the sum or difference

dividend the number to be divided

division finding the quotient of a dividend and a divisor

divisor the number by which another number is divided

E

edge the segment where two faces of a space figure meet

endpoint point at the end of a line segment

equivalent fractions fractions that name the same amount; *example*: $\frac{1}{2}$ and $\frac{2}{4}$

estimate to make an approximate answer rather than an exact answer

even number a number, such as 2, 4, and 6, that is divisible by 2

F

face a flat side of a 3-dimensional figure

fact family related facts using the same numbers

factors the numbers that are multiplied to find a product

flip moving a figure over a line to show a mirror image

fraction a number that names a part of a whole

frequency how often an event occurs

front-end estimation finding an approximate answer by using the digits in the place with the greatest value (the front-end digits)

G

graph a drawing used to show information

H

histogram a bar graph that shows the number of times data occur

I

identity element adding 0 to a number does not change the number; multiplying a number by 1 does not change the number—the number keeps its "identity"

identity property the product of any number and 1 is that number; any number divided by 1 is that number; any number except 0 divided by itself is 1

intersecting lines that have one point in common

inverse operations two operations with the opposite effect; addition is the inverse operation of subtraction, multiplication is the inverse operation of division

L

length the distance between two points

line a straight set of points that goes on forever with no endpoints

line of symmetry a line that divides a shape into two halves that are exactly alike

line segment a part of a line with two endpoints

M

mass the amount of matter that an object contains; the heaviness of an object

mean the sum of the addends divided by the number of addends; the average

median the middle number in a set of data

metric system a system of measurement based on multiples of 10 that uses centimeters, decimeters, meters, and kilometers, milliliters, liters, grams, kilograms; and measures temperature in degrees Celsius

minute a unit of time that equals 60 seconds

mode in a set of data, the numeral that occurs most often

multiplication an operation that uses two or more numbers (factors) to find the answer (product)

N

negative integer a whole number less than zero

numerator names the number of equal parts represented; the number above the fraction bar

O

odd number a number, such as 1, 3, and 5, that is not divisible by 2

open sentence problem in which a number is missing and must be identified

order the characteristic that items in a pattern have in common

ordered pair a pair of numbers that describe the location of a point on a grid

ordinal number a number that shows order or position

P

parallel lines in the same plane that never intersect

pattern a series of items or actions that appear or happen in a specific order

percent the comparison of a number to 100; *example:* 50 out of 100 is 50%

perimeter the distance around the sides of a polygon

perpendicular two lines that intersect and form four right angles

pictograph a graph that uses pictures to show information

place value the value of a digit based on its position in a number

plane a flat surface that continues in all directions

plane figure a geometric figure on a flat surface

point an exact location in space

poll a survey of the public or a sample of public opinion used to acquire information

polygon a plane figure made up of 3 or more line segments

prime number a number which has two factors, itself and 1

prism a 3-dimensional shape with similar top and bottom

probability how likely something is to happen

product the answer in multiplication

Q

quotient the answer in division

R

radius a line segment with one endpoint in the center of a circle and the other endpoint on the circle

range in a set of data, the difference between the greatest number and the least number

ratio the comparison of two numbers

ray a part of a line with one endpoint that goes on forever in one direction

regroup use 1 ten to form 10 ones, 1 hundred to form 10 tens, and so on

relationship the characteristic that items in a pattern share with each other

remainder the number left over after dividing

rounding writing a number as the nearest ten, hundred, and so on

S

second a unit of time; 60 seconds equals 1 minute

sequence the order in which the items in a pattern are arranged

slide moving a figure along a line (up, down, or over)

space figure a solid, 3-dimensional figure

square number the product of a number multiplied by itself

square pyramid a 3-dimensional shape with a square base, triangular faces, and pointed top

subtraction finding the difference between two numbers

symmetry a figure has symmetry if it can be folded on a line so that the parts match each other exactly

T

table list of facts in columns and rows

tessellation pattern of shapes that completely cover an area without overlapping or leaving gaps

tree diagram a picture that uses lines to connect drawings

triangular number a number that can be formed into a triangle using dots

U

unbiased random sample a set in which every member has an equal chance of being chosen

V

variable a letter used to represent a missing number in an open sentence

vertex the endpoint of an angle; the point where 3 or more edges meet

volume the number of cubic units that fit inside a space figure